Drowning in a sea of Family violence 〔...〕 〔alc〕oholic abuse, feeling abandoned by God 〔...〕 〔sev〕eral, Christa finally has her own 〔...〕 〔m〕ore drink just doesn't erase 〔...〕 〔...〕ce and abuse. An inveter〔...〕 〔...〕s story reminds us all that we are 〔...〕 of reclaiming hope even when desperately 〔...〕 to grab on to a most elusive and exclusive life in tne Hamptons.

In her final, desperate act of courage Christa finds in her own deepest heart, with the power of God to take charge of her life and with her children in tow, the ability to rise above the demons that have plagued her since childhood. It is a remarkable saga of one woman's refusal to be held hostage to the inevitability.

—**Marie Levine**
Author of *First you Die: Learn to Live
After the Death of Your Child*

Christa Jan Ryan knows why we have pain and what to do with it. In "Silent Screams from the Hamptons" she allows us to stand beside her as she shoulders Herculaneum pain. To let go of that pain is the challenge we all face. Christa has started with ending the abusive marriage, getting sober and seeking change in every facet of her life. Imagine all that energy going into loving herself and her children. Bravo Christa!

—**Jim Owen**
Meditation Teacher/Sound Healer/
Landscape Designer

With her latest novel, "Silent Screams from the Hamptons," Christa Jan Ryan proves once again that she is a whirling dervish with enough energy to light up Manhattan. An exterior made of steel and an iron will, she proves that adversities beyond anyone's worst imagination can not only be tackled, but risen above. Entertainment abounds as we frolic through the foibles of her millionaire clients. But, "Silent Screams from the Hamptons" is not your typical "get it off your chest" memoir. At its heart is Ryan's clear determination to create solutions that will work for people who are suffering through their own private hell.

—Joanne B. Carsley
Screenwriter of *Repeat Offenses*

We have watched God work powerfully in Christa, and our prayers are for her to continue to do his work, and be of service to those in need of her encouragement and inspiration.

—East Hampton Church of Christ

The strength of the heartbeat that threads its way through this book, only reflects how huge Christa's heart has become in feeling compassion for her fellow man.

—Dennis Watlington
Author/Screenplay writer
Author of *Chasing America*

Christa has a unique and compelling way of shooting straight from the hip.

—Betty Hill Crowson
Author of *The Joy is in the Journey:*
A Woman's Guide Through Crisis and Change

"Silent Screams from the Hamptons" is a poignant, sometimes hysterical, and mostly profound read. Christa bears her soul by sharing her journey with us. She is true inspiration for all who read this important book.

—T. J. Parsell
Author of *Fish: A Memoir of a*
Boy in a Man's Prison

Christa has articulately defined the gut-wrenching struggle of her internal battle between self-destruction and self-love. This book allows us the privilege of walking beside her to witness her journey to wholeness; and it forces us to look inside ourselves and contemplate where we are on our own path, and to take responsibility for where we are going.

—Steven G. Rise LCSW, BCETS

Silent Screams from the Hamptons

Christa Jan Ryan

Robert D. Reed Publishers
P.O. Box 1992, Bandon, OR 97411
Phone: 541-347-9882; Fax: -9883
E-mail: 4bobreed@msn.com
Website: www.rdrpublishers.com

Story development, editing, and additional material
    written by Anne McCormack
Editor: Cleone Lyvonne
Cover Designers: Cleone Lyvonne and Christa Jan Ryan
Author Photographer: Tim Lee
Cover Photos: Red Keyhole, © Lostbear from bigstock-
    photos.com; Key © Milosluz from dreamstime.com
Interior Designer: Amy Cole

ISBN: 978-1-934759-05-9
ISBN 10: 1-934759-05-8

Library of Congress Number: 2008924405

*Manufactured, Typeset, and Printed in the
United States of America*

Ten percent of all the Royalty's from this book will go to a fund that aids All Domestic Abuse Survivors.

The names and locations have been changed to protect my ass, period.

To My Good God who:
Is What He Says He Is,
Can Do What He Says He Can Do,
Proclaims I Am Who He Says I Am,
Has Made All Things Possible.

Dedicated to:

Christina Baker and Susan Caldwell

This book could never have been conceived
without their encouragement.

Acknowledgments

A special thanks to Meredith Hoffman, Maud Seaver, Barbara Ludlow, Joanne B. Carsley, and Anne McCormack for all their creative input, energy, and love that went into this book!

Without the professional and sensitive editing of the placement of material by Anne McCormack the birth of this book could have never happened. Working with Anne and all that we shared in common, helped open a door which allowed me to heal in a way I never thought possible. We may have written a book, but I feel as though I gained a sister.

There was a turning point in the final outcome of this Manuscript when Dennis Watlington, author of Chasing America, added his male perspective and knowledge to this story. His genuine interest and love added such a powerful dimension that I believe this book could never have held the power in its deliverance that it has without him. My love and Gratitude will always be with him. Thanks Dennis!

A note on forgiveness to all...

THE APPLE DOESN'T FALL FAR FROM THE TREE, AND ONE DAY YOU WAKE UP AND YOU ARE THE TREE

The mustard seed is the most prolific plant in the plant world. Ironically, in order to reproduce, the plant must die.

Table of Contents

Introduction.. *17*

Part 1: What Good Can Come From All of This Chaos? *21*

Prologue 23

Please Don't Let Me Grow Up to be Like
Mommy and Daddy... 27

Blues For the Redhead 35

Everything In Divine Order 45

Part 2: The Road to Hell is Paved with Deadheading....... *55*

You Take a Geographical Leap and You Wake
Up and Find Yourself.. 57

In the Cards 65

In Between Windmills and Millionaires 75

Mosquitoes In Paradise 85

All or Nothing at All 93

Lesson #1: Accepting the Things I Cannot Change 101

Brother Can You Spare a Mansion or Two?..................... 107

Lesson #2: When in Doubt, Run, Don't Walk 115

Lesson #3: Forgive But Don't Forget 121

From Cradle to Garden 129

Stormy Weather 135

Part 3: My Life Was Officially Out of Control *141*

Distractions in the Key of E-Minor.................................. 143

Is That a Light at the End of the Tunnel, or a
Freight Train? 151

It's Not the End of the World But I Can See the Edge 161

Of Love and War and Everything In Between................. 171

Calling All Angels 179

Shelter From the Storm 187

Epilogue.. *195*

About the Author.. *201*

Introduction

This book is about the Disease of The Family of Origin and how we unintentionally carry over our patterns of hurts, hang-ups, and habits into the next generation. The generational inheritance that I received was addiction and emotional woundedness. The legacy I wish to leave is how we can change our generational inheritance through the power of our willingness, love, and forgiveness.

The Importance Of Memory

I CAN'T GO FORWARD WITHOUT GOING BACK. I RETURN TO THAT VOICE THAT HAS NEVER QUIETED, ALTHOUGH SOMETIMES SPEAKS IN A LOW WHISPER. IT IS THAT LAST GASP THAT LONGS TO FIND PEACE WITH MY TRUE SELF.

A Memory

Ever since I could remember I was told that God never gives us more than we can handle. When I was little, lying in my bed at night and staring out at the stars, I believed this with all my heart. It made me feel warm when I was cold, secure when I was in doubt, loved when feeling unwanted and deeply cared for and special when there was no reason on earth for me to feel that way.

One night I remember seeing droplets of rain dripping down the window and believed God was crying, but I didn't know why and wished there was something I could do to make Him feel better. I jumped out of my warm bed and ran downstairs to ask my parents why God was crying; but before I could speak to them, I saw that they were crying too. They sat on the floor holding hands, in silence, just smiling through their tears at my three little sisters asleep on a blanket on the sofa. My triplet sisters had all been born with Cerebral Palsy.

I went back to my room, climbed under the now cold covers, and looked at the sky. I knew why God was crying. He was crying for my sisters, for my parents, and for the way His most divine creation had turned out. That night I was changed forever. That night I heard His gentle words come into my room and speak to me in a soft, loving, and caring way. Even God Himself could not make me understand how this situation could have happened to my family. He said, "I will always give you more than what you think you can handle, not because I want you to suffer, my sweet child, but always, always to remind you to depend and rely upon me."

1

What *Good* Can Come From All of This *Chaos?*

Take courage, the earth is all that lasts.
~ Sioux saying

Prologue

The Hamptons—Summer, 2000

I'm busting my ass working a shindig in East Hampton, while Jacob sits in his truck listening to tapes of his band's recent gig at the Memory Motel in Montauk. Our clients, *Big Bucks on the Hill*, are showing off their big bucks to four hundred of their closest big buck friends, as they celebrate the completion of their 1.5 million dollar waterfall on their Georgica Road estate in East Hampton.

I am beyond cranky but riding a champagne-fueled rush of glory over our latest landscaping triumph. Compliments have been flowing, along with the champagne from the Gucci-clad guests, for our work on the waterfall. It's Memorial Day Weekend, and I haven't had a day off since April 1st. I'm exhausted.

I grab a full bottle of Dom P and stroll toward

Jacob's truck as it gyrates to the beat of loud Rock 'n Roll. I watch him take a long hit from a joint before releasing a torrent of smoke.

"Hon," I say, "how about a little action before I leave for my mother's?"

"Yeah, sure, when I'm done," he says, looking annoyed. "Keep the bubbly chilled."

I head for the hot tub irked by Jacob's tepid response to my proposition. I watch as he suddenly leaps out of the truck to look at a sighting of bluebirds through binoculars. It's been some time since I've elicited as much enthusiastic interest from my husband. Undaunted, I fire up the client's tub and get into a sexy mood, hoping to take the edge off of my impending trip upstate to visit my mother. Mom recently had a massive stroke and is convalescing in a Kingston hospital. After waiting for Jacob for what seems like forever, I pop the cork and allow my heat to diminish, despite the tub's 104-degree temperature. I drain the entire bottle before passing out.

Several hours later, I wake up, hung over and shriveled, which induces a seething resentment at my husband who has left me to drown in my desire. I head to his truck, only to discover that he is passed out with a bottle of wine between his legs. I grab the bottle and empty the contents on his head. He awakens in a daze as I run to my truck, like my life depends on it.

As I put the truck in gear, I hear Jacob hollering, "You dumb, stupid, fucking bitch!" With wheels spinning, I hightail it off of the estate with the image of my red-faced, wine-drenched husband shaking his fist into my rearview mirror.

Two hours later I arrive at the hospital, and I'm filled with fresh anxiety over the illness that has befallen my mother. With a bouquet of Peonies in hand from an estate of one of my clients, I crack the door and watch as she presses the oxygen mask tighter to her face. I'm saddened by the thought that she will never again visit the beautiful gardens her daughter has designed.

I approach the bed and lay the flowers on her stomach before taking the hand of the woman who had endured the good, the bad, and the always crazy. Her face brightens and she lowers the mask below her chin. "Oh, honey, I was just thinking about you. Aren't these lovely flowers? Thank you."

As I sit rubbing both her hands, I can feel her old bones becoming my bones. She begins to narrate a story about the difficulty she had faced with my father bringing up triplet, handicapped daughters. There were six kids, and my parents struggled to raise us with little money and plenty of heartache. But I know that this blueprint wasn't what tore them apart—it was their abuse of drugs and alcohol. And it hits me like a ton of bricks: maybe Jacob and I were becoming more like my parents than I care to admit. Their alcoholic arguments were the soundtrack that echoed through my childhood. My young children are now listening to the same discordant music.

I gently rest my head on my mother's chest as she strokes my hair.

"I was thinking of something, Chrissy. Can I tell

you what it was I was thinking about?" my mother asks.

I look into her eyes and smile, holding back the tears that seem to have followed me my whole life.

"Of course."

She clears her throat and talks softly. I listen intently to what might be her last coherent words.

"You know, Honey, in 1948 I was working on a pageant down at the Kingston Redeemer Lutheran Church. I was conducting a choir and was told that there was a very handsome, young man working as a light manager. Well, he turned out to be your father..."

She drifts away for a moment and then continues with emotion, "Minna Elizabeth was a pound and a half and Maureen Ellen weighed in at two and three quarters. Michelle Ann was the fatty, about three pounds and a couple of ounces. They all went right into the incubator. I knew something was drastically wrong."

Her voice trails off and she begins to cough. I put the oxygen mask on her old face and tighten the elastic behind her thinning gray hair. I pull the blanket up to her neck, and memories hit me like a tornado.

1

Please Don't Let Me Grow Up to be Like Mommy and Daddy

Kingston, New York

Jeanne and Ernie Ryan met in church after the war. My father arrived home in Kingston, New York, after serving in the Air Force and got a job as a light manager at the church where my mother was directing a Christmas pageant. His eyes lit up when he saw Jeanne, and he asked her out for a drink. They fell instantly in love, and by that spring my mother realized she was pregnant. On Easter Sunday of 1949, they were married.

Jeanne lived by the rule, her rule: There was the right way, the wrong way, and Jeanne's way! She would rather be right than president. A graduate of Ithaca College, specializing in Physical Education, she had established her career as a high school coach before she met my father. Jeanne was one hell of a knock out—blond, buxom, blue-eyed, and beautiful!

Ernie Ryan was an easygoing person who went with the flow of Jeanne's way. When he wasn't selling insurance or wiring the electricity for Ulster Electric, he was unwiring himself at home, usually in front of the television. My father was tall at 6'4", extremely skinny, distinguished, and handsome. He was recognized with the Air Medal during World War II for flying missions during the Normandy invasion. He had survived the front lines in the war, but in our home Ernie was in retreat.

My parents formed a dynamic union of intellectual, spiritual, and creative chemistry. They shared a very powerful sexual attraction to each other. Mom always dressed to the hilt and that turned on my father. On Sundays they would get drunk and disappear into the bedroom for hours. We used to call my father Dirty Ernie because he was always pursuing mom for a quick squeeze.

My older brother Stevie was born December 8, 1949, followed by my sister Sandra three years later. The birth of the triplets was on November 13, 1955. It was a total shock. The doctor called to tell my father the news that his family had grown from two to five in a matter of hours. Dad went to sit down when he heard the news and completely missed the chair, ending up sprawled on the floor—an ominous sign.

Minna, Maureen, and Michelle were twelve-months-old when they were diagnosed with Cerebral Palsy, a birth defect of impaired muscular strength and coordination from brain damage, usually occurring during or before birth. The day of the diagnosis, Jeanne discovered that she was pregnant with me. That had to have been nine long months for my mother. I was born February 3, 1957, the sixth child in eight years.

We lived in a big old grey Victorian home with a wraparound porch that stood on the top of a hill on West Chestnut Street in Kingston. It was a dead-end street with twelve houses of practicing Catholics and no less than seven children in every household. At any given time there might be as many as forty-five kids playing unsupervised outside. We were a neighborhood gang, and there was always trouble to be found.

The chaos on the street matched the dysfunctional quality of life in our home. The hum of the washer, dryer, and dishwasher was ever-present and mingled with a continuous assault of radios, television, stereos, and screaming children. The noise level was beyond distracting. It always looked like a bomb had just been dropped. Our neighbor felt sorry for us and sent over her housekeeper, Rosie, to tidy up once a week. After Rosie was finished, we could never find anything and would rip apart the house in search of our belongings, creating even greater bedlam.

Jeanne was always running behind schedule, and half our childhood was spent waiting for mother. I have a wild memory of an incident when I was four years old. My mother dressed the triplets and me and placed us out in the old '52 Chevy that we nicknamed "The Bomb" to wait for her while she got herself organized for the day. As we sat in the car the triplets began rocking back and forth simultaneously.

After fifteen minutes, I was about to jump out of my skin from all the rocking. I leaped into the front seat to open the door to see what was taking my mother so bloody long. As I landed in the driver's seat, I accidentally kicked the car into neutral and we started to roll backwards. The momentum of the triplets rocking actually made the car roll faster. The triplets looked out the window and started to scream their heads off. "Wereeeer goinnng tooooo fast without youuuuuuu mommy!" yelled Maureen.

Out came my mother with a Pall Mall cigarette dangling from the side of her mouth. She saw the car rolling down the hill and bounded down the stairs three at a time. Jeanne ran like hell, driving the butt from her mouth, and surprisingly, her dentures became unglued and sailed through the air. My mother caught up to the car, opened the door, and jumped in. After gaining control of the car, she stuffed a cigarette into her toothless mouth and with a trembling hand managed to light it. "Myst 'ole Chrytie, shit, piss, and corruption!" she exclaimed.

My mother's life was demanding with a full-time job and a chaotic household. Every night my father buried himself in newspapers, and my mother was left with the Herculean task of trying to get six young children to bed at a decent hour. Jeanne struggled with her unmanageable situation until she couldn't cope and then would snap in a rage of anger that would send everyone, including my father, running for cover. We lived in great fear when her anger was unleashed and went to extraordinary lengths to keep her from going there. The siblings named her anger the "Big It." Once her anger was spent, it was always the same for my mother—remorse and regret. I learned early to manipulate her shame; it was the perfect time to ask for things that would generally have been denied.

With each outburst, my father disappeared further from the radar screen. The moment Dad came home from work, he camped out in a corner of the living room with his booze and cigarettes, disconnecting from the high-voltage energy circulating through the household. My father spent most of his time in an alcoholic daze.

My brother Stevie was brilliant. At the age of eleven, he was building go-carts and motorized bicycles from scratch. I have fond memories of watching him construct very elaborate models. He would throw away the instructions and under his breath would say, "I don't need those destructions." But he had learning issues and no interest in what school had to offer. I remember my mother insisting that "No son of hers" was going to be a blue-collar worker. It was unfortunate that the support he needed to help his budding abilities just wasn't there. His self-esteem was badly damaged.

Sandra was gorgeous. With her blonde hair and sparkling blue eyes, she was the belle of the ball wherever we went. She suffered with migraine headaches, possibly a symptom of her repressed rage for being put into the role of caretaker of the family. Mom desperately needed a built-in housekeeper/cook and Sandra was drafted for the job. She was overwhelmed with the workload at school and at home and stressed to the limit trying to protect us kids.

Our poverty was depressing. My parents could barely afford to put food on the table. I can remember Mom running out to the old "'52 Bomb" with a cigarette hanging out of her mouth and her checkbook in hand rushing to Central Hudson Electric Company because the power was going to be shut off by 4:00 P.M. How painful that thought still is to me of "The Bomb" racing down the road, and Mom speeding like a lunatic to pay the bill so that we had electricity for the night.

The triplets' disease drained the family pocketbook. It always seemed as though there was some crutch or mechanical device that was needed for the triplets. There was a constant buzz of "doing for the girls" and taking them here and there and in and out of hospitals and dealing with doctors. Between the ages of five and twelve, the girls went to a Cerebral Palsy Center and worked with therapists. And every so often Minna or Michelle would go in for an operation.

Minna was afflicted from her waist down and couldn't walk without crutches. On one occasion the doctors decided to cut her Achilles' tendon because they thought that it would help to stretch her legs and give her more mobility. That surgery seemed to produce no result, and to this day she is in and out of wheelchairs.

The right side of Michelle's body was severely damaged, with the left side being fairly normal. For the purpose of better grasping, one of the doctors thought to put a cow bone in between her thumb and her index finger in her right hand. Well, it didn't work. But it did traumatize her so much that she began coddling her cow-bone hand. Poor Michelle was extremely crabby and ornery and would lose control and have temper tantrums. We used to tease her and call her "the bullhead" or "Gimp-along."

Maureen and I played together the most because she was able to get around more than the other two girls. She was the least physically affected, despite her delayed mental motor skills and speech impediment.

Jeanne tried to foster an atmosphere of a Christian household. "Do unto others as you would want them to do unto you," would be the continual line that was repeated over and over as we would be beating the crap out of each other. "Mom, hold on, I'll be right there; let me do unto Stevie as he has done unto me!" I'd scream. It would drive her insane.

Dad stopped going to church even though the rest of us attended "religiously." He would sneak away on Sundays. Mom would ask, "Going to that God and Run Club, Ernie?"

She was referring to one of my father's favorite outlets: an all-male rod and gun club. He would hunt pheasants and deer with his cronies and hang out afterwards drinking beer and bullshitting about their kills. Joining this gun club had allowed him to run from the problems and insanity of our life at home.

The thing that detonated our dysfunction was my parents' drinking. Every night they would come home from work and my mother would mix scotch sours. It would start off so agreeably. We would hear the cha-chink of ice cubes in her sterling silver antique shaker and the sound of their amusing banter as the liquid was poured into glasses. After a few scotch sours, they would open the cheap sherry and port. As the night progressed, their raised voices would filter up to our bedrooms. We'd stick our heads under pillows, trying to quiet the inevitable knockdown, drag-out fight that would ensue. I would often awaken to the terrifying sight of my father punching my mother over the banister.

By an early age my overwhelming surroundings had ingrained within me a pessimistic view of life. Most of my thoughts during childhood were that life was JUST PLAIN UNFAIR! It was unfair that my sweet triplet sisters were handicapped, unfair that my parents were dealt such a heavy burden. Many times as a child, I would scream out: "GOD, WHAT WERE YOU THINKING? YOU WHO HAVE THE POWER AND GREAT HAND IN CREATION, YOU CALL THIS A PLAN? WHAT GOOD CAN COME FROM ALL OF THIS CHAOS?"

2

Blues For the Redhead

School was a place where I could forget my problems. I managed to get all A's in public school because of my inherent desire to learn, despite the fact that I was always in trouble. I found out early in my life that I could assume the role of something different than the sad life that "Christa" led. I was *the little brave redheaded squaw warrior*, a name I was given by my father, and spent many hours in a teepee in the backyard that I had made from a parachute Ernie had saved from his exploits in World War II. There I created a fantasy life of Christa, the Native American adventurer, which would shape the lies I told in school.

I found great comfort and solace in the outdoors with my father. An appreciation of nature was in our blood. He was part American Indian from the

Onondaga Tribe, located near the Finger Lake Region in New York. Dad would take me fishing and hunting and he taught me an appreciation for the outdoor life.

When I was eight years old, my father taught me how to shoot a rifle. I was intimidated as he picked a big leaf from a tree branch, placed it on my shoulder, and directed me to lay the gun across the leaf. As I felt the weight and length of the rifle, I closed my eyes trying to gather courage.

He started to laugh, "Oh, my little brave redheaded squaw warrior, how can you aim if your eyes are closed?"

"I'm so scared; can you hold it and I'll practice pulling the trigger?" I pled as I tried to hand him the gun.

"Oh no, little one," he cajoled, "if one is to be a warrior, one must practice the art of being a warrior."

I held my breath as I put the loaded machine to my shoulder, shaking and praying all the while. I looked through the scope, aimed the best I could, then shut my eyes and pulled the trigger. A noise rocked my essence and the power of the machine jolted my shoulder badly. I screamed in pain.

"Little brave redheaded squaw warrior, we are done for the day. Let's get you home."

I felt disappointed. I desperately wanted to be a part of his world; and if shooting a gun would give me access, and then I was determined to learn how to shoot. One time, while we were hunting, my father put down his rifle and said, "I'm going to tell you a secret. I carry a gun because it looks manly, but I really come out here to enjoy the scenery and the beauty, and most of all the peace and quiet." His weather-beaten face looked off into the distance, and he seemed to relax into the stillness of the air. "My sanity is being able to enjoy the great outdoors. My blood runs deep with my ancestors. There are messages in the wind and signs in the clouds and peace in the moment."

"WOW!" I thought, "Nature would settle the unrest that I was feeling in my soul. It was the only solution to the insanity and chaos that was my life." I latched on fast and tight to my Native American inheritance. Nature provided the conduit that would keep my insane life together and allow me to feel some peace of mind and heart.

I was a tomboy and had no interest in doing girlie things, like shopping and getting dressed up, and that worried my father. "You know, Christa," he said one day, "I don't know what you are going to do, but you can't go kayaking and canoeing and being an outdoor naturalist for the rest of your life." I was crushed that he would discourage me from following my heart, knowing the passion I felt for the outdoors.

Aunt Marion, my mom's only sister, employed me as her gardener when I was ten years old. She recognized the deep love I had for the outdoors and thought it would be a great idea to see if she could nurture the passion into a love for gardening. It worked! A connection was made between my love for nature and nurturing flowers, while channeling my excessive energy into a positive outlet.

Everyday after school, I would ride my bike to

work for her. This kept me out of trouble for the most part in the early years at school. Mom was always busy with coaching and after school activities. When school was over I wanted to get as far away as possible.

My aunt's next-door neighbor hired me, and before long several other neighbors did the same. By the time I was eleven, I had my very own business. I was able to buy any bike or any pair of skis and go wherever I wanted. I was waging my own successful war on poverty.

Minna was unusually bright for a handicapped child. She was the oldest of the triplets, the golden child in the eyes of everyone, and able to accomplish academics at the age-appropriate level. Minna had an incredible drive to achieve and was greatly frustrated by her disability. Her temper was legendary and she was capable of being violent. I once had to have five stitches after she hurled an iron bookend down a set of stairs and it hit me in the head.

Minna and my mother mixed like oil and water. She was not afraid of the "Big It" and would often refuse to comply with my mother's demands. She always seemed to throw a monkey wrench into the wheel at the most inopportune times.

One evening, I heard an ear-splitting scream from the triplets' bedroom. I ran to their room and watched my mother in a fierce struggle with Minna as she attempted to tighten a brace onto my sister's legs.

"You little difficult one," my mother hollered, "You will do as I say!"

"Stop it, PLEASE, let's skip tonight!

Mom grabbed Minna and wrenched her braces as tight as she could as Minna screamed and struggled to free herself. "For Gods sake, someone help! She's going to hurt me!"

The "Big It" unfurled. My mother slapped her across the face. "I'm going to show you who runs the show in this household," she roared. You could hear a slight slur in my mother's words. Suddenly, she grabbed her full glass of wine and poured it down Minna's throat. Minna gurgled and spat but swallowed a significant amount. No sooner was it down her throat than it came back up again, and she proceeded to vomit all over my mother. I watched in horror as Sandra came to the rescue.

"I really do think it's time for you to get your rest," Sandra cooed at my mother. "I'll put everyone to bed. Why don't you quiet down in your room?" My mother burst into sobs of uncontrollable remorse as Sandra led her from the room. "It's okay, Mom. Everything will be okay," my ten-year-old sister consoled. After comforting my mother, Sandra returned to clean up Minna and sing us all to sleep.

If the "normal" siblings had a difficult time coping with the dysfunction, what was it like for the triplets? They were aware of the alcohol-induced toxicity in the air and could sense when the atmosphere became emotionally unsafe. What I wouldn't have given to be a fly on the wall in their bedroom at night, to hear the conversations that floated between the three of them.

I pleaded to God continuously, THEY'RE JUST

HELPLESS HANDICAPPED CHILDREN. WHY AREN'T YOU HELPING THEM GET BETTER? I CAN'T UNDERSTAND ANY OF THIS! I'M ONLY A CHILD MYSELF.

My mother was the "Great Pretender" and would act as if everything was fine. Jeanne was an active speaker and often gave talks to civic groups about Cerebral Palsy. She considered herself a feminist and liked to wax poetic on the profound questions of life. I could always tell when she was about to launch into profundity. She would take a couple of hits from her scotch sour, clear her throat, and assume the righteous certitude of a minister.

"Chrissy, if you are going to live in the world, you are to accept all things, with all people, at all times." This was a favorite quote from Karl Marx. She was very impressed by Martin Luther King, Jr. "We all have a dream," she would often say. "We must be lovers of all nations, lovers of all skins, lovers of all people."

I would bring her back to the problems of our family. "If we're lovers of all people, how come you and Dad were so mean to each other last night?"

My mother's pride and inability to ask for help kept her in a deep state of denial. "Our family isn't perfect, Chrissy. We have more to bear than most. Considering conditions, we're doing pretty well up here on the hill."

"But Mom," I would say, "why do you cry so much after you lose your temper when you and daddy are fighting?"

"Oh baby shakes," she would respond, "that's how all married people act."

I didn't believe her. Anger and alcohol were the coping mechanisms for my parents. Any time the stress level escalated, you could anticipate arguments, and big doses of alcohol to numb any responsible reaction. We lived under a cloud of some looming tragedy that would take us by surprise. At an early age I was scared to death and started to question God. It was impossible for me to comprehend why I was constantly being thrown in these horrific situations with adults whose behavior didn't make me feel safe.

In 1968, when I was eleven years old, Jeanne was prescribed Valium. It was not unusual to find my mother unconscious on the bathroom floor. We knew the drill: call for an ambulance to take her to the hospital so she could have her stomach pumped.

One evening, I was alone in my bedroom listening to my parents having a terrible fight. Stevie arrived home, came into my room, and wearily fell onto my bed. As we were talking, we heard my father's rifle cabinet open and the frightening sound of a gun being cocked. Stevie and I bolted downstairs, and there he stood staggering back and forth in an alcoholic meltdown with the gun at his head and my mother screaming.

"Please, Ernie, put it back. It's okay. We'll be okay!" she pleaded.

Stevie lunged at Dad and knocked him to the floor as I jumped on his chest and grabbed the gun out of his hands. My brother led my father up to bed as my mother wailed hysterically about her children witnessing this tragic episode. The next morning it was as if nothing had happened. My father had no memory of the incident and my mother was firmly in denial. Who would believe the horror I was living?

There were many nights that I laid in bed wanting my life to be over. I was so overwhelmed with not knowing what to do or who to talk to about this insanity. I spent many hours entertaining the image of my mother's Valium in her medicine cabinet, playing a suicide scene in my mind over and over again.

"Today should be the day," I thought one morning as I waited for everyone to leave the house. I walked toward my mother's bathroom and reached into her medicine cabinet for the Valium bottle, willing myself not to think about what I was doing. I poured the pills into my hand and calmly began swallowing them one at a time. All the while, I looked at myself in the mirror and saw my young face and thought this is the answer to all of my pain and confusion. I AM TOO YOUNG TO SORT OUT ALL OF THIS!

My mother found me that afternoon and knew instantly what had happened. She put me to bed to sleep off the drugs. Jeanne didn't want to risk taking me to the hospital. There would be too many questions from the authorities on why her eleven-year-old child was into her stash of Valium. When I regained consciousness, I was in my bedroom. My brother was crying as he stood over the bed holding my hand, pleading desperately with my mother. "Please, take her to the hospital now."

I opened my eyes and looked at my mother.

GOD, WHY AM I STILL HERE WITH THIS CRAZY WOMAN! YOU'RE STARTING TO PISS ME OFF!

"See, she's awake!" my mother said. "Christa's going to be fine. See Stevie, I knew God would watch over her; she didn't need to go to the hospital after all."

My brother walked away crying. The incident was never brought up again.

3

Everything In Divine Order

Sandra and Stevie graduated from high school and left home. I felt abandoned and in acute pain at having been left alone with my parents and sisters. I was emotionally paralyzed and pleaded endlessly with God: PLEASE HELP ME! SHOW ME HOW TO FIND A LIFE THAT IS WORTH STAYING ALIVE FOR! I was twelve years old and desperate beyond words.

I discovered that a shot of bourbon helped brace me for whatever was going to happen that day and began drinking daily. High speeds took me out of my pain zone. I became obsessed with skiing, biking, rock-climbing, and with anything or anyone that offered me a cheap instant thrill.

I was out of control with my drinking during school ski outings. My friend's Italian grandfather made wine in his basement, and we would smuggle half-gallon wine flasks from his stash for our trip. On one of our excursions a new English teacher, Greg Classen, was the chaperone. He was handsome and well dressed, with dark Mediterranean features, and was considered cool by all the popular kids. He was a new teacher who was working toward tenure. There were always rumors about Greg chasing female students. I set my cap on being the girl he would flirt with on this trip.

I started showing off my talent for high-speed gymnastics on the slopes. Greg was trying out his ski legs for the first time and was impressed with my skill. I began giving him helpful instructions and aggressive flirtations. At the end of the day, Greg suggested that we plan our own private ski trip together. I was desperate for attention and thrilled that an experienced, educated man was showing an interest in me.

Greg and I continued to flirt with one another and meet secretly during school. I began to dress with more care, squeezing my ninety pounds into sexy mini skirts in the hope that my twelve-year-old athletic body would be attractive to him. We met in between classes and after school when he would be tidying up from his workday. I would throw myself at him by constantly bending over so he could see down my shirt or up my mini skirt. Greg would lose control and grab me. "Baby you make me want to do naughty things to you." I was a virgin and overwhelmed by his seductive overtures.

He wanted to take me on a ski trip and I agreed.

I told my parents that it was a school-sponsored trip, and they gave their permission. Greg picked me up in his Fiat convertible one morning at 4:30 A.M., and we headed off to Vermont without suspicion. The conditions were spectacular on the slopes and we skied all day. The excitement seemed to heighten his attraction for me. "Girl, I'm so hot for you," he whispered. "You turn me on like no other." We were making out and it was very different from my experiences with groping thirteen-year-old boys. I was thrilled that someone found me irresistible.

Late that afternoon, I stood in the lobby of the hotel watching Greg check in and felt a wave of alarm pass through my young body. WHAT AM I DOING? He suddenly looked old. When Greg turned toward me and flashed a lecherous smile, I knew I was in trouble. He grabbed me by the hand and led me toward the room. I didn't know how to tell him that the deal was off. In the room Greg suggested that I take a shower first. That sounded great; it would give me time to plot my escape. I stripped off my ski clothes and stood under the hot water with my heart pounding in my chest. He came in the bathroom, and I heard him lock the door behind him. "Shit, I should have done that!" I thought. Next thing I knew, he was in the shower soaping me down.

"I'm done," I said casually as I stepped one foot out of the shower. "It's your turn." He grabbed my arm and yanked me back into the shower. "Hey," I protested, "that hurt."

"I'm sorry, baby. I just didn't want you to leave."

"Please, Greg," I reasoned, "I'm only twelve. I don't think I'm ready for this."

"Christa, you're not leaving me hanging now. It's gone too far." He turned off the shower.

"Please, please, Greg. I'm just a kid," I pleaded desperately.

"You little bitch. You said you wanted me. Now shut up and follow through!"

He grabbed my arm hard and yanked me out of the bathroom. I was terrified as Greg threw me down on the bed and held his hand over my mouth. I tried to scream and bit his hand. He hit me in the stomach, which knocked the wind out of me, then tied one of his socks around my hands and gagged me with the other. I lay on the bed and felt all of my power leave my body as he raped me.

When he was finished, he rolled off of me and I quietly sobbed. "I'm all you've got now, little girl," he coldly stated. "Nobody will want you now that you're no virgin."

I lay in the bed waiting for him to fall asleep, feeling violated and ashamed. GOD! ARE YOU OUT THERE? WHAT JUST HAPPENED TO ME AND WHY? When I was sure that he was unconscious, I carefully slipped out of the bed and got dressed. Never had I felt so alone. I found a bus going to Kingston and rode home feeling devastated, full of regret and remorse. Even at so young an age, I understood that I had lost more than my virginity. I had lost a big chunk of self.

We avoided each other at school, and I kept my mouth shut. The repressed rage and hostility I felt towards him was too large for my mind and heart to comprehend. I started to drink more, mixing vodka with my mother's Valium to accelerate the buzz. I stuffed the whole violating experience away in a cloud of chemicals, pretending that what I was feeling wasn't really justified.

At fourteen, I fell in with a group of kids who did not meet my mother's approval. They were fun-loving, wonderful athletes from Port Ewen, the wrong side of town. My mother nicknamed them, "The Port Urine Crowd." But in the end Jeanne relented and allowed me to hang out with them because we played sports together, and my mother was grooming me to be an athlete.

I excelled in relay races, shot put, and broad jumping and won the Presidential Award four years running. My new friends were into partying as much as training. I continued to drink, take uppers and downers, mushrooms, and smoke marijuana. My mother was suspicious that I was indulging in substances. "Did you take your pot today?" she would ask. "Yeah Mom, two pots, one clay and one plastic," I'd slyly quip, eluding the inquiry. Whatever her objections, it was easy to get out at night. I just had to wait for one of my mother's alcoholic blackouts before slipping off to meet my friends.

I started to have a romantic interest in Ameous Alve Lucas, a basketball player who was African-American. Our relationship quickly became hot and heavy. Ameous had a beautiful smile, a fun-filled heart, and we both loved to dance. His parents were professors at New Paltz University, and they didn't seem to have a problem with our relationship. Ameous was very smart, and we would do homework together after school. It was a classic, healthy boyfriend/ girlfriend relationship. He was genuinely attracted to me, but sexually inexperienced. I felt safe with him.

A rumor had circulated around school that I had been involved in a thing with Greg. Now I was dating a Black student. I was developing a reputation for being loose and fast. Teachers were concerned and students thought I was out of my mind. I wanted to live up to the rumors. *Fuck you all! Try to beat this one, baby. First a teacher, now a black boy! Match that, if you dare.*

Ameous and I decided to go to the prom together. I hadn't told my mother about my relationship but didn't expect any problems. Jeanne was progressive for the time and constantly preached tolerance. "You do not judge a man by race, creed, or color." My mother's life was a train wreck at home, but when she walked through the school where she taught and coached, she was respected. She loved her students, particularly the African-American athletes, many of whom were so talented that they were an inspiration to her. She believed they were going to be future Olympians and poured a lot of energy into her prize athletes.

"Mom, I'm going to the prom with Ameous," I said as she was pouring a scotch sour into a glass. There was a heavy pause, and I thought I detected a flash of pink cross her cheeks for a moment.

Finally, she said, "No, you're not! No daughter of

mine is ..." She stopped speaking.

"Is what, Mom? Going to go out with a black boy?" I shouted at her. "You are such a hypocrite! Practice what you preach."

I had no idea that I was dropping a bomb. Obviously, integration was fine for my mother as long as it didn't include her daughter's dating choices.

"You have to leave right now," she dismissed me. "I have nothing to say to you. I still might not have anything to say to you tonight, but I'll think about it and talk to you tomorrow."

I stood in the kitchen and felt a wave of nausea in my stomach from the smell of her scotch sour. "Do as I say, not as I do!" I shrieked. "You are just a racist hypocrite!" I ran from the room.

The next day she reluctantly gave me permission to go to the prom with Ameous. When Ernie heard the news he screamed, "Oh my God, Jeanne!" But the decision stood.

At this point my father had just about had it with everything—with my mother, the triplets, me, and life in general. He was having an extramarital affair and would leave home from time to time. Then he would move back in and life would resume, as we knew it. No one ever talked about it, but it was a common occurrence. My father's affair increased the battles between my parents, and I could no longer stand to live at home. I fled to Sandra's house on Eastern Long Island. Sandra had married quickly after graduation from high school and had two children. I refused my mother's demand to come home, unless I was permitted to attend a boarding school.

She acquiesced, and in 1974 I began attending the Oakwood School in Poughkeepsie. I fell in love with the school and did very well academically. The school reactivated my passion for the outdoors. I exchanged track and field for rock climbing, kayaking, and hiking the Appalachian Trail.

I became inseparable friends with Jenny Schubert. She and I were known as the Southern Comfort Girls because of the large quantities we would consume when "tying one on." Jenny was brilliant. She had scored a 1600 across the board with her SAT's and earned a full scholarship to Penn State University. She was the bright and shining star in my life.

Jenny's family was very well respected in Kingston, with her father being a lawyer and her mother a doctor. She had this little green Fiat, a present from her parents on her sixteenth birthday. They were the Have's and we were the Have Not's. And yet, we'd spend many an afternoon tearing up the ski slopes together.

One weekend during my first semester, I went to visit my father at the Electric Store, his place of work. I was shocked when I saw his face. He had been brutally beaten with blackened eyes and swollen cheeks.

"What happened?"

Ernie proceeded to tell me several days earlier he had broken the news to my mother that he was leaving her for another woman. My mother's rage overwhelmed her and she picked up a broom and attacked him. He tried to defend himself by grabbing the broom, but he was no match for her ferocity.

With a defiant lift of his chin, he said, "Moving out is the only choice."

"How is Mom?" I asked.

"She's so angry that I'm afraid of her."

He gave me a light hug before turning away and resuming his work. His bruised face suggested that things would never be the same again.

With my parents on the brink of an alcoholic abyss, I experienced a moment of clarity: There was no one in my life who could offer me the support I so desperately needed. I headed back to school, a safe haven that protected me from the chaos. But chaos had a way of tracking me down.

One night at the end of my senior year, a group of us decided to go drag racing down Chandler's Drive. Jenny rode in her boyfriend's car and I in another car. With alcohol fueling our engines, we began to race, battling neck and neck, maxing out on youthful delirium. Suddenly, tragedy struck when Jenny's car flipped over multiple times and began to smoke. In a panic, we circled back and the sight of bodies moving outside of the car provided a momentary reprieve. But as we drew closer, I knew that something was drastically wrong. The numbers of bodies didn't add up. I started screaming, "Where's Jenny?"

Our car had barely come to a full stop when I bolted out to run over to the smoking car. Jenny was in the back seat, crushed between the console and passengers seat. I screamed for help, but I knew that Jenny's life had ended.

I started to wail before bursting into a full-blown rage: GOD! YOU TOOK THE WRONG FUCKING KID! SHE HAD EVERYTHING GOING FOR HER AND I HAVE NOTHING BUT MY DRUNKEN FAMILY. WHY DIDN'T YOU TAKE ME?

I didn't go to the funeral. Instead, I cried for days and stayed wasted on Southern Comfort. Soon after graduation, I left Kingston in hopes of never returning. I was intent on building a stone wall around my heart. At age seventeen, I had lost everything that mattered to me in my life. I fell into an emotional blackout that would stalk me for thirty-five years. I had concluded that there was no God.

2

The Road to *Hell* is Paved with *Deadheading...*

We are nature too.
~ Shakespeare

4

You Take a Geographical Leap and You Wake Up and Find Yourself

Sag Harbor, 2003

I am sitting at the bar of the American Hotel in Sag Harbor drinking their best fifteen-dollar-a-glass Zinfandel and thinking about the AA meeting I have just attended. Mary L led the meeting and shared about her childhood growing up in an alcoholic home. Her story was sad and familiar. She spoke with the grace and self-assurance of a practiced storyteller. Near the end of her qualification, Mary's voice unexpectedly cracked. The room hung on her every word as she described a funeral she had recently attended. It was for her forty-one-year-old sister who had died from full-blown alcoholism. The moment sent a stabbing pain into my heart as I thought, "It could be my sister Sandra." I rushed from the church basement to my spot at the bar. Now I sit drinking my wine, trying to make sense out of my irrational behavior, when something congeals in my soul. My sweet sister is sober. Sandra has been in recovery for several years. I'm the problem. I've been sitting in meetings for nine months debating the facts of my alcoholism. I can be Mary's sister. I'm forty-four-years-old and my life is in danger if I don't face up to the truth—I'm an alcoholic. I put down the glass and walk out the door.

East Quogue, Long Island

In the spring of 1978, I headed to Long Island to be near Sandra and found a job in a greenhouse on the North Fork. It was just a spot on the map as far as I was concerned, far enough away from all the pain, misery and suffering that I had endured. My plan was to start life over again: a new job, a new place, a new me.

At the greenhouse I met Dot Carter. I was instantly struck by her remarkable resemblance to Jenny. They were both blond, blue-eyed, milkmaid specials. Dot was a gifted landscape architect and was working part-time to get through the winter months. She and I picked up where Jenny and I had left off. It was through this friendship that I started to heal from the pain of Jenny's devastating death.

The greenhouse business slowed down in the late spring and Dot was returning to work for her father's landscaping business. We had become such close friends that the thought of not continuing to work together never entered our minds. Dot introduced me to her father, Rich Carter. His eyes lit up when he saw that I was a redhead, and he offered me the job.

Rich Carter owned a zillion-dollar landscaping business. I felt like I had finally arrived. As much as I had enjoyed working with flowers in the greenhouse, my real desire was to be outside. My Native American instincts continued to seek the peace and tranquility that only the open space of the outdoors could bring. My childhood had ordained that I be functional in chaos—good training for this job. There was plenty of madness in the world of East Quogue Landscaping.

I was engulfed in a business of men and machinery transforming the earth. I witnessed the tremendous visual changes that could be accomplished by a big-time landscaping operation and was instantly hooked. Poking around in gardens with a few pansies lost their appeal when I felt the earth move under my feet. I wanted to ride this horse in a big way, and Rich loved the idea that I had a take-charge mentality.

One of my first lessons while working on the east end of Long Island was that macho men on their macho machines could be trouble. This was very evident one day when Dot and I, weeding in the vegetable gardens of a large mansion, saw a huge crane with a bucket dangling from its appendage grinding its way across the property. We ran for cover as the gigantic mechanical beast bullied past, wiping out the entire garden, and leaving in its wake a cloud of smoke and fumes. The beast was followed by four ten-wheelers filled with enormous rocks. The workmen were putting in a waterfall and a pond. The bulldozers and backhoes came through next, dangerously close to the pool house. The "bulldogs" then began tearing up the hill, and the next thing I heard was a deafening boom. The pool house exploded.

"Great," I'm thinking to myself, "what's next?" Pressure in the gas line had created the explosion. The driver jumped off his machine, came running over to me and yelled, "Can you get in the main house?"

"Sure, I can get in the house," I replied.

"Then call up Lilco, and tell them that we need somebody to get over here and turn off the gas, immediately!"

"What are you, nuts? The whole house will blow before they arrive!" I snapped.

"How soon can you turn off the gas line that services the pool and hot tub?" asked the worker, now nervous because he wasn't sitting atop the safety of his "intimidator."

When the police and fire engines arrived, they were concerned that there was a live gas line that could have blown up the entire house.

Accidents were all to commonplace. Workmen who were hung-over, or just had bad attitudes, plowed and destroyed anything that inconvenienced them. My experience at Carters was not only a lesson about landscaping at its finest but always a life lesson of how to interact with all types of people. They taught me all of the big-time do's and don'ts of the business. I was addicted to the pace, atmosphere and excitement in a huge way.

I worked with a very close-knit group of guys, who I grew to love and nicknamed "Carter's Seven Dwarfs." One day the dwarfs were grading a hilly area at a house in Southampton. John Brown, a tractor operator, dug into the earth a little too deeply, scraping off two septic tank covers, before driving half the tractor into the tank. John was thrown from the tractor and grabbed on to the septic tank rings. We were all horrified. This was a life-and-death situation.

He was holding on for dear life as we rushed to help him. But we were too late, and he slipped and fell into the tank. John screamed for somebody to drop a rope or do something. All the guys were moaning, "Man, it stinks. Oh, that's so gross." The smell was indescribably foul.

"What the hell are you doin'!" I screamed. "Get a shovel over here! Get a rope over here! Let's go! He could drown in the shit!"

The dwarfs were bending over, getting sick to their stomachs. I'm thinking to myself, "Man, this is a really bad sign. These are his friends, and all they're concerned about is the smell!"

Finally, one of the workmen dropped a rope with a shovel into the hole. After pulling John out, the only words anyone could muster in relief were, "Oh, man, you stink."

Meanwhile, the tractor was ready to fall in the tank at any second. Nobody was paying any attention. The guys were still yelling, "Oh man. Oh God, this is really gross!"

"Guys, let's move the tractor out of here before it goes in the tank." I pleaded. "Someone, get on the tractor!"

No one responded. Dot jumped on the tractor and popped it in reverse. She started driving the tractor slowly out of the tank, moments before it would be swallowed by the shit pit. Later, we always had some good laughs over that one. John Brown became John Shit Brown forever more.

Dot and I were two women on the loose in a man's world. Most of our work was with male contractors, and we used our feminine wiles to our advantage. We were inveterate flirts and would continue the games after hours at nightclubs around the Hamptons. *Scarletts* was a famous disco in Westhampton Beach where we loved to dance and drink all the guys under and over the table. But we also took care of each other and always made sure we brought each other home at night. That was the unspoken understanding.

As Dot was studying for her degree in Landscape Architecture at Cornell University, the Carters encouraged me to go for my degree in Landscape Management at Farmingdale University. As I learned about blueprints, plant selection, and working with crews, Dot was becoming a brilliant designer, one of the most gifted landscape architects I have ever met. She would come home on breaks and share all of her newfound knowledge about landscaping and was my best teacher.

Through my education, I learned that the basic purpose of landscaping is the creation of a pleasant, functional, and personal environment. I would visit dozens of exquisitely designed gardens and talk to their owners and to landscape architects. I began to see landscaping and gardening as an art form. Each garden was planned in some detail before a plant was bought or a brick was laid. I felt I was contributing with my work by improving the quality of day-to-day living.

Dot's parents bought her an old boathouse that was being moved from Quiogue to East Quogue so that when she graduated from Cornell University she wouldn't have to pay rent. I was starting to get a glimpse of what Dot was accumulating and what I was not. I was still working on a low salary, and I knew that there wasn't much of a future with the Carters for me. They were set with the management end of the business. They needed Indians, not Chiefs. I would have my landscape management degree at the end of the year, but I wondered how far it was going to take me. I wasn't sure if it was going to be feasible for me to really make a living out on the East End?

The idea of moving up to an area near Boston, Massachusetts was enticing. I would be closer to the ski resorts and to my sister Sandra who had recently moved and was now working for a horticultural lab in the city growing test-tube orchids. Sandra found the perfect condo for me outside of Boston that was near a nursery and landscaping operation. I put in a few applications in the Natick/Framingham area and did some interviews. I started tinkering back and forth with the idea throughout the winter. I was about to be twenty-four and had this burning desire to start doing something with my life.

5

In the Cards

The bigger collision I have with people, the stronger the destiny.

Dot and I sat in the high bleachers in Madison Square Garden in the winter of 1979 at a concert for Jethro Tull. Dot was mesmerized by the hypnotic jazz-rock of their signature song, *Aqualung*, but I was having a difficult time sitting still and decided to take a walk. I slithered my way across the aisle making apologies, until my leg got tangled in some knees. Losing my footing, I took a header and landed in the lap of a very handsome cowboy. I couldn't have planned the fall any better.

"Gosh, so sorry, wasn't watching myself. Please forgive me." Baby blue eyes the color of robins' eggs silenced my apologies. I felt my stomach go into freefall as I was hypnotized by his handsome face. A go-tee surrounded a beautiful smile and offset a soft gentle face that was looking at me intently.

"Baby, you can fall on me anytime." We looked like we belonged together. He was wearing a brown rawhide fringed cowboy jacket and cowboy hat, while I had on my tight Sassoon jeans and cowgirl boots. His long legs comfortably cradled my small frame. It took all of my effort to break the spell and make an attempt at collecting myself. He guided me to my feet, and I felt the power and firmness in his hands.

I took the seat next to him and we introduced ourselves. His name was Jacob Durite, and I thought I would die when he told me that he had a landscaping business in the Hamptons. I don't remember hearing another note of the concert as my attention was diverted to this lovely man for the rest of the evening. It felt like divine intervention.

The conversation flowed effortlessly. He had been living on eastern Long Island for a little over a year and had struck gold instantly with his business. My ears were ringing as he talked about his life in the Hamptons. He had a jazz show, *Take Five,* on the local radio station, WBBX, and co-hosted a television show, *Living with Nature,* that he also wrote, produced, and edited. Jacob was a musician and played bass, guitar, and keyboard for a local band and had played for the Paul Winter Consort.

"He is so brilliant and smart," I thought. Who cared about Jethro Tull? I had hit the jackpot. He was handsome, creative, the perfect age, and owned a landscaping business. I went for it! I looked into his handsome face and said, "If this is a dream, don't you dare pinch me." He laughed and responded, "I wouldn't think of it, Baby." As the music flowed over our heads, we found a mutual unspoken understanding that words could not possibly formulate.

We made plans for later in the week. The night of our first date lived up to all of my dreamy expectations. I set the scene with music and candlelight and prepared a fabulous dinner. Jacob arrived on my front stoop wearing his favorite cowboy attire—blue jeans with a jean shirt, a rawhide-fringed jacket and an imposing cowboy hat. He walked with an "I'm hot shit" strut, looking very musician cool, and smelling as though he anticipated a score. From the moment he stepped through the door, the conversation flowed effortlessly. We ate and filled each other in on the details of our lives.

Jacob was twenty-eight years old and had been born in Massapequa, Long Island. He attended State University at New Paltz, not far from Kingston. He loved the area, and after graduation decided to settle and open a natural food restaurant. Jacob and I discovered that we shared a mutual love for Lake Mohonk located in the Shawangunk Mountains, where I had grown up hiking, rock climbing, and hunting.

We talked shop, and he recited the Latin names for a variety of plants, exhibiting a horticulturist's vocabulary that I was just beginning to acquire working at Carters. I was beyond impressed. Here was a man who shared my love and passion for working and living in the great outdoors. As we spoke about our work, I felt right then and there that I had found my soul mate.

As the hour grew late Jacob began to fondle me on the couch, kissing my neck very persuasively, and whispering in my ear, "This has been a perfect evening. Let's not end it." But I didn't want to rush into bed with him. I let him get aroused before cutting him off and leading him to the door.

"Another time."

"You're throwing me out. I can't drive like this," he moaned.

"Put it on cruise control, Romeo. You'll be fine."

We started going out twice a week. One of our favorite things was to go to Ron Campsey's *New Moon Cafe* in East Quogue and listen to jazz and play backgammon or chess. I was the better chess player, and he liked that. I'm ruthless and competitive beyond words. As an athlete I had been trained to put it all out for the big win. He would eat pecan pie and laugh at the intensity of my desire to win.

I trusted him implicitly. There was nothing that I didn't share with him. For the first time in my life, I let down the guard that had been the Great Wall of China that protected my heart. Jacob reminded me of my dad. I was aware that some part of me was drawn to him in order to heal from my broken relationship with my father.

I was invited to hear Jacob's band play in a bar

called *Snugglers*. When I arrived at this smoky dive in Amagansett, he was on stage wearing sexy ripped jeans and a nice shirt rocking his heart out. He looked hot, and he knew it. I jumped on to the dance floor and felt myself being carried away by the music. I was getting turned on watching Jacob play his guitar. It was an erotic experience.

The night was on fire, and we went back to his crash pad in Springs—five bedrooms for five guys. The place was a mess, but by that hour I was oblivious. We had both been drinking, which heightened the expectation of consummating our relationship.

"Baby, there is nothing I won't do for you," he whispered as he undressed me. "You are an angel sent down from God."

His compliments swept me off my feet and made me feel special. When he touched me, my body came alive as never before, unleashing something that I didn't know existed. We had sex for hours.

The next day we drove into town, and I fell in love with the beautiful little village of East Hampton. The town prided itself on maintaining a clean, classic look. There were colonial houses with white picket fences, pristine churches, and ultra chic boutiques and shops along Main Street. Jacob brought me to several of the places where he was working. He had six very rich clients, and I was blown away by the extravagance of the accommodations. My work at Carter's was beginning to look like a training ground compared to the extensive landscaping projects Jacob was juggling.

I immediately recognized a great opportunity.

The green in my eyes saw dollar signs. It was the chance of a lifetime. My organizational mind could excel in this business. It seemed overwhelming for one person to handle, particularly since Jacob was juggling the work with his radio and TV shows, and his nature and bird walks.

We went back to his place and fell into bed to discuss business, but his interest was focused on what was happening between the sheets. When I persisted, he laughed, "Baby, you can run the whole damn show as long as we do lunch-hour right here in bed." He was ready to give me anything as long as I was willing to hop in the sack. Where do I sign! I didn't get back to my own place for four days.

I decided to give Rich and Dot Carter my fond farewells. I graduated from Farmingdale University on a Thursday and got on the Friday morning train headed for East Hampton. Jacob picked me up at the train station and we drove through the "fabulous Hamptons."

The towns, villages, and hamlets that make up the Hamptons include Amagansett, Bridgehampton, East Hampton, Montauk, North Haven, Sag Harbor, Sagaponack, Southampton, Springs, Wainscott, and Water Mill. Each had a distinctive flavor of its own. I was captivated by the formal beauty of the East Hampton Village streets, and intrigued by the alluring fields of Wainscott. We had lunch in a restaurant nestled on the bay in the historic whaling port of Sag Harbor. The Atlantic Ocean beaches were just a short distance from the bays and inlets of the Long Island Sound, and there were water views everywhere you turned. I was thoroughly seduced by this idyllic atmosphere.

The Hamptons have long been a summer getaway for the rich and famous. Mega-millionaires live on gorgeous estates with stately homes, tennis courts, swimming pools, and pool houses bigger than the average family home. Their multi-car garages house BMWs, Mercedes, Rolls Royces, and Jaguars—all necessary for survival in the Hamptons.

I told Jacob that I was coming to work *with* him, not *for* him. I had learned so much from East Quogue Landscaping, and I was going to show him how it should be done! Jacob had the ability to charm the snake charmer's snake. People found him trustworthy. He was the initiator and would generate the business, and I was the follow-through person. Jacob seemed relieved to have somebody step in and help negotiate, manage, manipulate, problem-solve, enable, gain control, and reorganize. It was an insane business with a very limited amount of time to earn your dough. I vowed to work until I dropped. We would make lots of money and be a complete success. *Mmm...I was going to have to rethink this whole God thing. Maybe he wasn't such a bad God after all.*

The pace of spring on the eastern end of Long Island goes from zero to a hundred miles an hour in a blink of an eye. You can feel the frenzy in the air as the season begins. April 15th to October 15th is the set amount of time in which to make enough money to get through the winter months. This is the time when we had to perform.

During the six-month season, I pictured myself as an airplane speeding down the runway with the engine at full throttle, and I am flying, flying, flying at an intense speed. During the season you can't skip a beat. Most workweeks encompassed ten to twelve hours a day, seven days a week, and required being on call twenty-four/seven. If we lost a day because of rain, we'd work from dawn until dusk to be able to complete work that was promised in the spring. There is nothing worse in East Hampton than being known as someone who can't deliver. You can overcharge your client and you can be overbooked, but you can't take on work and be unable to fulfill the requirement.

We set our adrenaline dial for the big push to Memorial Day, the do-or-die weekend. You have to get the main work done by that weekend, even if it snows right through May. That's the expectation. Through spring, there is frenzy in the air.

My first day working in East Hampton, Jacob and I barreled in and out of nurseries picking up annuals. "Do you get a discount when you buy from these places?" I asked. "Oh, it's not worth it," he replied and gave me a long explanation about buying plants that clients inevitably decide they don't want. "What would I do if I bought wholesale," he asked, "buy huge quantities and then sit on them all?"

Right away it hit me that Jacob wasn't spending the time it took to take the clients to the nursery to pick out exactly the plants they wanted. I saw that there was a wide margin for correction. But not this first season... maybe the next.

In the Hamptons everybody was in a big rush to get it done yesterday. One of the comments we consistently heard from contractors was that celebrities were extremely difficult. They had a reputation of being scattershot. After implementing their choices, they would invariably change their mind and want a complete overhaul. "By the end of the day, please."

The celebrities also had a reputation for not paying on time. Your bill went to the house manager, then to the bookkeeper, and from there to the accountant, and on and on. Contractors seem to be living on air, waiting for checks to come in for work completed months earlier. The parking spots at the post office were clogged as we routinely stopped to see if there were any checks in the mail. If the checks were in, we'd race to the bank before it closed. Most of us were overdrawn. We've paid insurance bills, the IRS, and sales tax, but haven't been paid by our wealthy clients yet.

I started looking at how Jacob was running his business and what his methods were for getting paid. I told him that we could run a smoother operation with an organized payroll system and a specific schedule for the workers, instead of just winging it. I got busy setting up schedules with both the workers and the clients.

I was in the saddle, controlling the reins, throbbing with an intense energy that bordered on obsession. Jacob encouraged me. He would stroll onto a job site stoned and look over my work, full of compliments and affection. The more I proved my value, the more he was able to pay attention to his true passions: music and birds. It was a good arrangement.

My life was exciting, exhilarating, and breathtaking. Jacob had a red phone in his apartment, the hot line I would call it. I knew when that phone rang it meant money in one form or another. It would either be a client, a friend about a music gig, or a possible drug score. Off we would go at the moment's notice. Jacob had a sparkle in his eye and a passion for life. For an ambitious, poor, young woman with a chip on her shoulder, his attention was quite exciting. From the time we woke up in the morning until we hit the sack at night, it was nonstop, high-impact all the way.

6

In Between Windmills and Millionaires

Jacob had accumulated an astonishing group of clients; some were among the wealthiest people in Manhattan. There were captains of industry, movie stars, film directors, fashion designers (including Calvin Klein), Michael Cimino, Dudley Moore, Juan Tripp, Stephen Ross, Martin Revson, Gabetti's, Paul Simon, Donald Bruckman, Alan Slifka, Peter Tishman, to name a few! I wouldn't have traded working this circuit for anything in the world. To be a fly on the wall in the lives of these people was quite an experience. I got a bird's eye view on how the rich and powerful live and play.

One of our first celebrity clients I'll call Mrs. Goldstein, a very funny person and wonderfully enthusiastic about her gardens. She and her husband had bought a mega-mansion and asked us to re-design the gardens to her specifications.

When I showed up with my crew to begin planting, Mrs. Goldstein emerged from her house wearing adorable designer overalls and a sexy gardening hat. She was in costume and ready for action.

"I really want to get my hands dirty," she enthusiastically informed. "Show me what needs to be done." This was the last thing a landscaper wants to hear. But I do love to teach people about gardening, and so I worked with her that day and listened patiently to her not-so-practical suggestions. Big mistake!

The following weekend when I returned, I immediately sensed that something was wrong. "It's July 4th weekend," I thought. "What happened to the Astilbe that was in bloom last week? Where are the Japanese Irises that are supposed to be blooming?"

I realized what Mrs. Goldstein had done and it hit me like a ton of bricks. I just gasped and started to cry, "Oh my God! She deadheaded all the new buds."

Mrs. Goldstein came out of the house as proud as a peacock to show me all the work she had done.

"See, isn't this just great?" she proclaimed. "Look how clean the garden is. Last Sunday, oh, I can't tell you how great I felt. I spent the whole day in the garden. It was heaven! I pay my therapist $250 an hour and he can't come close to transforming me the way working in the garden can!"

"Mrs. Goldstein," I said, "I think we need to talk. The garden does look really clean. But don't you notice anything missing?"

Stupid moron, you cut off every single flower in the garden.

I spent the rest of the season trying to salvage her garden by planting annuals to replace the perennials she had beheaded. At the end of the summer came the phone call telling me how unhappy she was with my services.

"You were a great inspiration initially," said Mrs. Goldstein, "but unfortunately, I question your ability. At the end of the day, your work did not live up to expectations."

I learned a life lesson from this experience. From that point on, when a client asked if they could help in the gardens, I had a little speech: "I take zero responsibility for being your gardener if you decide to rearrange things without me." And when asked why that was I would respond, "The road to hell is paved with deadheading."

It wasn't long before I had my first encounter with almost running over a rock star. We had three clients on West End Road, a street leading to Georgica Pond from the east. One payday I was flying down the road, way behind schedule, unaware that I had left my clipboard on top of the hood of my car. Mr. Super Rock Star happened to be pushing his daughter in a stroller alongside the road. I swerved to avoid hitting them and my clipboard, holding paperwork and four checks totaling close to twelve grand, went sailing through the air like leaves in the wind. I pulled over and got out of the car.

"I'm so sorry. Please, please accept my apology. I was driving too fast."

I looked at the most famous lips in the world as they enunciated in a thick British accent.

"Girl, I believe you lost your papers."

I didn't care all that much about the paperwork. I have a memory like a steel trap. But I was frantic about finding the checks.

Mick Jagger's graceful smile took me by surprise. He was extremely nice and joined in the search. One of the biggest rock stars on the planet was on hands and knees looking through the underbrush on my behalf. It took us a good fifteen minutes to collect everything. I thanked him profusely and reached out to shake the hand that wrote "Honkey Tonk Woman." We chatted a bit and he introduced me to his little girl in the stroller. He was renting a house on West End Road for the month of April. I told him that the off-season was the best time to be in the Hamptons.

"Oh, yeah," he replied. "I've been out here in the summer and it's a nightmare. No parking spots, horrible lines, and crowded beaches. Oh, to be out here on a warm day in April... it's paradise."

"You know what?" I said. "It is paradise."

We shook hands again before we parted. At that moment, I thought that I might not wash my hand for the rest of my life.

Jacob and I were responsible for the maintenance and upkeep of large estates. We supervised independent contractors in charge of the lawn mowing, pool cleaning, housecleaning, etc. We were always in the car driving from site to site, the part of the job that nearly drove me crazy because the traffic in the Hamptons was overwhelming. During the summer months, it is a tourist-infested free-for-all that swells to the breaking point and the roads are chaos. My impatience screamed, "I need to make money, damn it!"

I wasn't prepared to have traffic control my schedule so completely. The quality of drivers in the Hamptons exasperated my last nerve. This was my territory, and they were going to have to play it my way! I drove like a bank robber fleeing the cops.

Contractors and people like me are always in a big rush, and the roads become our battlefields. The average contractor zooms at 65 to 75 miles per hour, knowing what stop signs we can slide through and where the speed-trap scanners are set. We juggle our personal business on cell phones while careening down the middle of the road, passing on the right, and gunning it, losing wood, plants, tools, and "you name it" off the back of our truck beds. Whatever is flying off is flying fast and furious. God forbid we slow down; we'd be losing fifteen or twenty minutes of checking on whatever needs to be checked on!

The clients seemed happy that I had come onboard. I was very attentive to their needs. Their expectation levels were extremely high. They didn't want to hear about the particulars of delays and snafus with the irrigation system or the pool heater. They could afford to have everything taken care of...yesterday.

Maybe there was going to be a bright side to the hell I had endured in my childhood. Having grown up in a highly dysfunctional family, I needed to live in a very organized and structured way. These people loved being enabled, and I saw an opportunity to take control. I was definitely in my element now! *Sure I can take care of you. I can take care of anything. You want your chickens delivered from Iaconna Farms? No problem. We'll just call up old Sal and order them. You want your blueberries and raspberries from Round Swamp Farm? No problem.*

Friday was shopping day and I started making the rounds to the farm stands so that our clients didn't have to take any time out of their busy schedule of tennis matches, massages, Botox treatments, gallery openings, and dinner parties. I could have everything dropped with their housekeepers at their doorstep. I would pick flowers and arrange them in bouquets for all the rooms.

Taking care of our clients' needs was a full-time job and then some. I worked nonstop and set my aspirations high. The harder I worked, the more fulfilled I felt, and the more the money rolled in. I realized that I had an opportunity to succeed beyond any of my dreams. My thirst for more was unquenchable. It was protection from the trauma of my impoverished childhood.

Jacob and I had very different working styles. While I was extremely ambitious, he worked at a much slower pace, which included time-outs, sitting in the truck listening to various NPR stations, or chasing birds with his binoculars. I was so in love, I chose not to notice how much these interruptions affected the flow and focus of our workday.

Jacob described himself as a high-quality "minimalist" with only a pick-up truck, a handful of help, and the occasional power tools. He cultivated the Japanese concept of mind, body, and soul, balancing the energy flow of the gardens with a meditative tone of working with the earth. He thought that I overdid everything.

We were quite a pair. I was bouncing off of walls in a frantic race to overachieve, while he never missed an opportunity to drop everything in order to watch a rare bird in flight. Storm clouds might have been on the horizon, but our business was growing well, our clients were happy, and we were making tons of money.

"Ladies and gentleman, welcome to Take Five." I watched Jacob through the glass window of the control room as he caressed the microphone with his melodic voice. He had a Sunday night jazz radio show at Southampton College that was nicknamed, "Sit back, take five, and watch all the cars head west." I would go with him to the station and bring all my accounts receivable and any paperwork or bills that needed to be done while he was on the air.

It took me a while to understand this whole jazz thing. I had never even heard of Dave Brubeck. My only jazz experience consisted of watching my parents bopping around to Glenn Miller's "In the Mood." One

Sunday afternoon he started off the set with the album, *Jazz Samba,* featuring Stan Getz. I stopped what I was doing to really listen. I was spellbound. It was like falling in love, passionately. It was sexy, romantic. I felt like the blind person who could now see.

Jazz scored our sex life, supporting wonderful passionate moments on sultry, warm evenings. Jacob's love of music was one of his greatest gifts to me. Our mutual love for the music produced our best times together.

My relationship with Jacob was a very intense, physical one. We made love two or three times a day. Lunchtime consisted of food and wine or beer. Afterwards, we would go to a private area on the estate, spread out a blanket and enjoy each other, before taking a short nap. Several times we had been caught in the act by the odd butler, driver or cook. Jacob was attentive and considerate and would surprise me with unexpected gifts and beautifully written love songs that swept me off my feet.

As I spent more time in the Hamptons, I realized that there was an interesting paradox at work on the East End. A person with a high set of morals could definitely succeed, but a person with a substantially lower set of morals could succeed even more.

I saw plenty of ways that the wealthy Manhattanites could be taken advantage of in short order. Arriving in the countryside, stressed and strained from the city, they were eager to establish personal relationships with the gardeners, carpenters, and electricians that worked for them. They craved the openness and honesty of country people who they felt they could trust. They wanted to hand an open account to their workers and say, "Could you get me this?" or "Could you charge this at the hardware store?" Once you had earned their trust, they seemed genuinely naïve to the fact that they were leaving their accounts open to larceny.

Plumbers and carpenters were charging for copper piping when copper piping wasn't put in, or charging for grade-one lumber and not using grade one. It was also happening with the gardening and landscaping business. What client was going to count how many pansies you put in or petunias you planted, or how many geraniums went into a pot with the ivy? It was a test of morals and ethics.

Despite the dysfunction in my family, we were raised with the golden rule. There didn't seem to be any ethical code in this part of the world. I knew that I was trustworthy and that at the end of the day I had to live with my conscience. I knew, too, that Jacob and I wanted to be successful, wanted to climb up that ladder, maybe two rungs at a time. We wanted the house, the cars, and the vacations. We wanted it all!

But the longer I lived in the Hamptons, the quicker I got sucked into the mentality that it would be easy to overcharge for everything!

I saw drugs and alcohol running rampant in the trades, and it didn't take long for Jacob and me to fall into the daily routine: work hard, party harder. We buckled our seatbelts tightly and prepared for the wild ride on this train of opportunity powered by greed and overindulgence, with our addictions getting fed fast and furiously! Money, sex, and booze! But there was little time to include emotional or spiritual intimacy with each other. We let it rip. Live fast, Die young, and Leave a Good Looking Corpse.

Landing three new clients at the beginning of the season allowed us to buy a new truck, close up shop for the winter and head off to the wine country of California for five weeks. Returning from California, we started our second season eager to sock money away for retirement funds and the next big trip. After having spent the first season with the majority of all the clients, I had an overall sense of what pleased them. I had also ventured out and got a hold of wholesale growers to help us cut down on the overhead. We had upgraded our client list by twenty-five percent. That was a big jump. But we were young, ambitious, and anxious to keep the money rolling in.

7

Mosquitoes In Paradise

The real estate boom really started taking off in the 1980's. Jacob's father continuously told us, "If you're going to get serious about your business, you better find a place in East Hampton to live." During this time we'd been driving the commute from my place in East Quogue.

Renting out east was nearly impossible for the average working person. Year-round rentals were hard to find, and getting into a winter rental only meant you'd have to evacuate for the summer. Landlords could get more money renting to out-of-towners from Memorial Day to Labor Day than they could all year from a local, so they had no incentive to rent for the year.

Jacob and I somewhere along the line had gotten it in to our heads that it would be a great idea to buy ourselves a 25-foot sailboat that we could live on in the waters surrounding East Hampton. We rented a slip at Sunset Cove Marina, outfitted "The Stray Cat" with everything she needed, and we were home. Jacob and I fell into a nice routine: after work we would shower at a client's house and finish off the day with a sunset sail. We'd grab a bottle or two of wine and something for dinner and in no more than five minutes out of the slip we'd be in paradise.

"Top me off, Luvy," Jacob would say, using his pet name for me, "so we can feel the breezes of the wind gods." I'd refill our wine glasses and say, "Here darling, to the wind, wine and the women; long may they carry us." We were right out of a Bette Davis film, notwithstanding the hokey dialogue. It was unadulterated fun and freedom from our life on land.

New to the sailing world, Jacob and I had plenty of virgin voyages. One time we found ourselves trying to sail with the jib upside down and ended up completely high and dry for hours waiting for the tide to come in. After several mishaps, we soon mastered the science of reading the charts. Sailing became my solace. When I had that tiller in my hand and we were ripping through the waves with the wind perfectly hitting the sails, I felt like there could be nothing wrong in the world, nothing wrong with me, nothing wrong with anything.

One of the many things that attracted me to Jacob Durite was the fact that, unlike me, he seemed to come from a *normal* family. His parents, who had summered in a cozy little cottage on Three Mile Harbor since the early 1960's, had been married for forty-two years. His father was a beer salesman and his mother was a school secretary. They seemed like lovely people.

As time wore on and I got closer to the family, I started to understand that there was no warmth or physical communication among them. There didn't seem to be any kind of expression of emotion or compassion. Sympathy was a word that was not in their dictionary.

When alcohol was in the mix, there was no telling what might happen. One occasion at a family Father's Day outing, Jacob's father had a few too many Rob Roys and latched onto one of his annoyances, Jacob's choice of career.

"Hey Pal," he said to Jacob, "when are you going to stop tinkering around in peoples' backyards and get serious about making real money. That job is for sissies!" He was stubbornly ignorant to the benefits and profitability that the landscaping business offered.

"For crying out loud, Dad," Jacob's brother John chimed in, "you don't even know what they do? They have a wonderful business. Don't be so critical."

Jacob's father jumped up and grabbed John by the shirt and said "You God damn loser!" He then went into a full-blown rage and screamed at us, "You're all a bunch of fucking losers as far as I can tell. God damn it!"

Everyone scrambled for cover as Jacob's Mom gingerly approached him. "Ron, you're spoiling the day. Everyone is here to be with you?" He turned on her and blasted, "You dumb stupid fucking bitch!"

I was embarrassed for Jacob's mother that she would be subjected to such awful language from her husband in front of everyone. But this would become typical holiday fare at the Durites, with Jacob's father standing in a rage pointing his finger at everyone. I bent over backwards to accommodate him, but we stayed losers in his eyes forever.

An important part of our landscaping business involved holding hands and patting heads. This meant not only being creative and inspirational but also encouraging the clients to be excited about their own ideas as well. Constant reassurance was needed. "Everything will be wonderful when it's completed. You're a great client. This project is going to be the most fabulous in all of the Hamptons."

Schleppie Silverman came to us as a referral. He was a gay gentleman, in his sixties, from real old money, and had an adorable place up in Northwest Woods. Schleppie wanted to do a complete renovation, gut the entire property, and add a pool. It would be an enormous amount of work.

As Jacob and I approached this new project, I sensed trouble. Our initial survey of the gardens was done with Schleppie and his lover, James, a handsome, pleasant man in his mid-twenties. We walked around the estate and listened to their ideas. Schleppie and James got in a few snits about their difference in opinions. "Well, I thought we had decided that this is what we were going to do," moaned James. *Oh God! It's going to be one of these appointments. Get out the crystal ball. We're going to have to read their minds and try to figure just what it is that they really want.*

Later that afternoon Jacob and I were waiting in the living room. Almost every single piece of furniture in the house was constructed out of authentic animal horns. The lamps had horns to support the shades, the tables had legs made out of horns, and the bedposts were horns. Everywhere horns, horns, and more horns. You had to have a good dealer who knew how to hunt down this eccentric type of furniture.

As we surveyed the room, we heard Schleppie yelling, "James, put that cork in the bottle. You are going to share that wine with our new landscapers." A slightly inebriated Schleppie staggered into the room to greet us, followed by James who carried a tray of glasses and wine. James stumbled on one of the tables and the tray went flying.

"God damn horney table!" James exploded. "I told you not to put the table there, James," Schleppie snapped, "You idiot!" James grabbed the spilled bottle of wine and began drinking from the bottle as Schleppie went into a rage cursing his lover. Jacob and I just looked at each other and rolled our eyes. He grabbed Schleppie and escorted him out into the gardens as I dealt with getting James back together.

The more time Jacob and I spent working with this *odd couple*, the more apparent it became that drinking was a big part of their lifestyle. Even when we arrived early in the morning, they often reeked of alcohol. We frequently found ourselves in the middle of rip-roaring fights between the two of them. There was nothing that could be brought up for discussion that didn't lead to an argument.

One morning we arrived for work and Schleppie greeted us at the door with two big, black shiners. "What happened? Are you all right?" I asked in shock.

"James hit me. I really need a drink."

"It's 9 o'clock in the morning, Schleppie. How about a cup of coffee?" I asked. I looked around and saw cabinet doors hanging off their hinges and huge holes in the walls. Schleppie sat there crying.

"What happened?" Jacob questioned with a bewildered look on his face.

"James put my head through the walls. Oh, I'll be all right; just put a little Kahlua and some vodka in the coffee."

I sat with him and heard the rest of the story. Each time he took a sip of the laced coffee, he got madder. He had given James full run of his credit cards and bank accounts, and James had cleaned him out to the tune of a half-million dollars and then hightailed it back to Canada.

What do you say to somebody like this? *You gave him that kind of access to your accounts?*

"Oh, I'm so sorry, Schleppie," I said, remembering that the customer is always right, even the stupid old fools.

A week later we drove by and saw a "For Sale" sign on Schleppie's front lawn and that was the end of that job.

We didn't view this type of behavior from our clients as unusual. Drunken behavior and fights were nothing out of the ordinary for Jacob or me. We had both been raised in alcoholic, violent homes. As the early romantic glow of our courtship settled into a committed partnership, a power struggle began to emerge.

Time constraints required us to juggle clients, and Jacob and I could never agree on a priority list. I was the practical one and wanted to give preferential treatment to the clients who were the quickest to pay. Jacob was thinking about whatever bird he had last spotted and where in town he might find it. As I worried about paying the bills, he was blissfully unconcerned and doing his thing. Our relationship was slowly slipping into a worrisome pattern of arguments and apologies.

One evening I was waiting for Jacob at the dock. I had fully stocked the boat with beer, champagne, wine, and a beautiful dinner and planned for a moonlight sail. Jacob had stopped at his Dad's and was taking an unusually long time. I became impatient and began drinking without him. When he arrived, I was too drunk to notice that he was very upset and lashed out at him.

"Where the hell have you been? Dinner's cold." Jacob lost it. He began smashing the beer and champagne bottles on the dock.

"Don't you see I have enough to contend with already?" he screamed. "You dumb stupid fucking bitch!"

I couldn't believe he had said that to me.

"You sound just like your father. Don't blame your problems with him on me," I retaliated.

A rage flashed across his face, and I saw a part of him that scared the hell out of me. Jacob threw me down in the cockpit, and to my astonishment, began punching me in the ribs. He then whacked me in the face and only the blood spurting from my nose stopped the beating.

"Don't you ever call me my father!"

Jacob collected his stuff and left me alone sobbing my heart out. I was devastated.

How could he have done this? I blamed myself for drinking too much and starting the fight. After cleaning myself up, I proceeded to go out and get absolutely shit-faced. Jacob came home in the wee hours and woke me with remorseful passion. We communicated in the language we understood: lovemaking. When we awoke the next morning, we pretended that nothing had happened.

8

All or Nothing at All

Valentine's Day, 1984

I cooked for the holiday: shrimp cocktail followed by champagne chicken, baked asparagus, and roasted potatoes, accompanied by two excellent bottles of chardonnay. For dessert, we had my freshly baked berry valentine pie, coffee, and a couple of snifters of cognac. At the meal's completion I felt more than a little drunk and very content. The candles on the table cast a dim light over the room as we sat quietly sipping the last of the cognac, listening to the sorrowful sounds of Miles Davis' trumpet.

As he lifted his long lanky body out of the chair, Jacob said, "I've been waiting for this moment all night." All of a sudden, he was on bended knee in front of me, removing a jewelry box from his jacket. He took my hand and spoke. "You know you're the one for me. There could never be anyone else. You're my everything." He slipped a beautiful diamond on to my finger. "Please say that you'll marry me."

He had taken me completely by surprise. For the first time in my life I was speechless. I sat silently with a stupid grin on my face. Finally, I managed to open my mouth but the words sounded distant. "When do you want to do this? How? Where?" He smiled a little drunkenly and said, "It doesn't matter, Luvy, just say yes." He leaned into me to give me a kiss. My emotions were firing alarm signals. "What's the matter with you?" I thought. "You love this man." I settled into the familiarity of his warm mouth and slowly my uneasiness quieted. At the end of the kiss I had tears on my cheeks. "Jacob, I would love to marry you." He took me in his arms. My dueling emotions of happiness and terror played ping pong in my stomach. I wasn't sure that I was ready to make this commitment.

But that didn't prevent us from taking time off to go on a two-and-a-half-week honeymoon trip to Europe. It had been my idea to try the honeymoon first! We spent a couple of days in Paris before touring the wine regions in France, traveling to Champagne, Alsace, and Rhine, and lastly down to the Beaune area. My doubts about the engagement were sedated by the romantic charm of the French countryside.

The wedding and reception took place September 16, 1984 at the 1780 House in East Hampton. The Durites and the Ryans descended on the Hamptons a week prior to the wedding—and, no surprise, they did not like each other.

The Durites were conservative Catholic and unhappy about the non-traditional ceremony we had planned. Ron Durite, Jacob's father, was very vocal in his criticism. First problem was that Jacob and I had taken our honeymoon before the wedding. Very improper to his way of thinking as was my decision not to invite Jacob's very overweight niece to be flower girl. Then we were getting married on a Sunday, instead of Saturday. Finally, he was horrified that we were going to be married outside by a minister and not in a church by a priest. Nothing was happening by the book, and Jacob's family took it very personally.

Jeanne arrived in town with great fanfare, playing the mother of the bride for all it was worth. After several years in an out of rehabs, my mother had finally gotten sober. She looked beautiful, as always, and expected to be treated with due deference. Right away, mom went into control mode—attempting to rearrange my plans to fit "Jeanne's way." I wasn't having any of it. Jacob and I were paying for the entire wedding. "Mom, you are a guest at my wedding," I confronted her. "The arrangements are none of your business." Her face colored slightly, but she remained silent.

My mother had rented two cabins in the marina for herself, Maureen, Michelle, Sandra, and Stevie. Having avoided all family intermingling for years, Minna refused to attend. Other than the occasional Thanksgiving, we had not been together for years. The triplets were in assisted living and working at a rehabilitation center. Sandra was working as a lab technician. Stevie was living in a house given to him by mother that she had inherited from her Huguenot connection.

It was tense—years of bad vibes and unresolved emotion were bouncing off of the walls. Everyone was mad at everyone else. Sandra and my mother had not spoken for years. We were, not surprisingly, a dysfunctional bunch.

Sandra, Stevie, and I bonded around several bottles of booze. We went out partying in the trendy Hamptons' nightspots. When we returned, the "Big It" greeted us.

"You're all drunk!" my mother bellowed. "What the hell are you doing?"

"We're all right, Mom," I said, "just doing a little sibling bonding," after which the three of us collapsed in laughter. My mother in the throws of *IT* hurled accusations and objects: shoes, books, pillows, an alarm clock came flying. We were laughing hysterically before running out of the cabin.

My mother's recovery from alcoholism consisted of attending one Alcoholics Anonymous meeting and declaring that she had gotten it. But that didn't stop her from offering plenty of program advice the next morning at breakfast. As Sandra, Stevie, and I nursed hangovers, Jeanne preached. "You must go to Al-Anon to deal with your co-dependency. You all need ACOA meetings." We rolled our eyes at each other and said, "Yeah, sure, Mom. Whatever." Mom no longer had any control at this party.

It was the wedding week from hell, a three-ring circus. Just when I thought things were as bad as they could get, my father arrived with his long-time mistress Laura. By this time Dad was a very sick man. His alcoholism had advanced to the point where he was incoherent most of the time. He and Laura stayed at an Inn in Amagansett, out of my mother's firing range.

Meanwhile, Jacob's problems were mounting with his family. They spent the week trying to talk him out of marrying me. The Durites disliked my family on sight. They focused their disapproval on the fact that my father was living with his mistress, but they were scornful of the whole lot of us. Jacob and I were having constant arguments, and three times the wedding was cancelled.

On the night of the rehearsal, the two families gathered; and you could feel all of the tension of the week coalescing. After the rehearsal, the Durites planned to host a dinner. Responding to the chilly breeze from the groom's family, Maureen whined, "Why aren't they talking to us? Why isn't anyone introducing themselves?" My mother decided to take action, and she approached the Durites to engage in a little friendly conversation.

After a few cordial moments, Ron complained, "Why can't they get married on Saturday?"

My mother scoffed. "So what! Christa has never conformed."

"Well then I don't have to support this marriage. And I won't. The dinner is off!"

He grabbed his wife and stormed out of the room. Something in me snapped as I watched my in-laws drive away, leaving the wedding party hungry and mystified. "I'm going to pull this wedding off," I vowed. "I'm going to show you all. Nobody messes with me!" If not for my defiance, the marriage might never have happened.

Hurricane Diana whipped through eastern Long Island the next day. If the wedding had been on Saturday as Ron Durite desired, it would have been a disaster of fifty-mile-an-hour winds and driving rain.

The following day as a baroque trio played Mozart, one hundred and fifty friends and relatives gathered on the patio of the elegant 1780 House. Four marble stairways lined with boxwoods lead down to a sunken garden. We had designed an altar covered with chrysanthemums on one of the stairways where the ceremony would be performed.

My mother was dazzling in a pink ensemble: chiffon dress, pill hat, satin coat, and spiked high heels. Ernie was drinking non-stop and incapable of escorting me down the aisle. We had seated him in a chair by the altar.

As I took my first steps toward the stairway in an ivory 1890 cocktail dress bought in an antique store upstate, all of the tension of the week slipped away. This was my wedding and I planned to enjoy myself. I walked gracefully toward my inebriated father. He rose carefully and took my arm to escort me the final steps to where Jacob and the minister stood. Dad smiled sweetly and kissed me gently before handing me off to my husband-to-be. Jacob and I had written our vows with the assistance of the minister, and we recited them flawlessly. Suddenly, we were pronounced husband and wife.

Jacob and I had a great time at the reception. People danced, ate, and drank. The afternoon flew by as we made the rounds to all of the tables. I finally had an opportunity to sit with my mother. We watched Jacob across the dance floor as he talked with a member of the band.

"He reminds me of your father," she said wistfully.

"I know, me too," I answered.

"I think it's a good match."

At that moment my father walked very unsteadily across the dance floor on the arm of Laura. Anxiety clutched my heart.

At the end of the reception Mr. Durite stood up and announced, "Anyone wanting a real meal and real music is invited to my favorite restaurant on my tab." An uncomfortable silence spread around the room. The color faded from Jacob's face as he absorbed the verbal jab. Jacob's brother confronted his father. "Please don't ruin this occasion, Dad." Ron turned crimson and grabbed his son by the throat before landing a right hook to the jaw. "I'm sick of you losers telling me what to do!" Ron hollered.

This final insult signaled the end of the party and people began departing. I went to Jacob's side and put my arm around him.

"Nothing I do pleases him," Jacob said mournfully. "Success, marriage; I'll never gain his respect."

He was crushed beyond words. There was nothing I could say. I gave him a hug.

"I'm here for you now," I said.

At the end of the night, we sailed into the sunset towards Block Island with several bottles of Dom Perignon and a few wedges of cheese. Jacob's father had put a damper on what had been a wonderful day. After making love, I lay awake listening to the sound of Jacob's breathing. My stomach was uneasy from too much champagne and a sudden panic attack. I was afraid that I had made a terrible mistake in marrying Jacob. I suppressed the thought, tucked it into an open file from my childhood marked denial.

9

Lesson #1: Accepting the Things I Cannot Change

A few months later, I received a phone call from my brother telling me that Sandra had been in a car accident. She had bruised a few ribs and was in a neck brace. I immediately suspected that her drinking was to blame. I was informed that Sandra had driven the wrong way down a one-way street and had slammed into a fire hydrant. She left the scene of the accident with her car sitting atop of spewing water.

As I drove to the hospital I thought about all of the problems that alcohol had created for my family. Mom was finally sober, but my father was on a suicide mission with his daily drinking. In the past couple of years Stevie had received three DWI's, and Sandra was always carrying drinking warrior wounds. The triplets had been addicted to prescribed medication for years and it was taking its toll. I left the hospital heart-broken for my sister, but convinced that my drinking was tame in comparison to the rest of my family.

In May of 1985, we gathered again for another wedding. My father had made the shocking choice to marry Laura. After the ceremony, my father and Laura stood in a receiving line accepting congratulations. I felt uneasy and waited at the end of the line, and by the time my turn came I was sobbing uncontrollably.

"Baby shakes," he consoled, "be happy for me. I love Laura. Please, bless this union."

"But Dad, if it is truly the best thing for you, why do you look like hell! You look like you're ready to die!"

"Oh Christa, you were always the worrier. Put your fears aside today and let's go eat, drink, and enjoy! Have faith my little brave redheaded squaw warrior."

I was not comforted. My sense of impending doom was powerful.

One month later I received a hysterical call from Sandra. Her words were garbled and I couldn't understand anything she was saying.

"Sandra, get a hold of yourself! What's the matter?"

"It's Dad."

"What about Dad?"

"He's in the hospital," she cried.

"What happened?" I demanded.

"I don't know. He's in a coma and the doctor said that he's going to die any day."

Since his wedding, I had been waiting for the call. He had gone into the hospital on the previous Saturday for blood work, and by Sunday night he was slipping into a coma.

I immediately dropped everything and went to Middletown Hospital. Everyone was there taking turns sitting with my father. Mom went in first, but my father was so uncomfortable in her presence that he tossed and turned until Sandra and I asked her to leave. As we waited in the corridor for her to say her final goodbye, my father began a loud, sorrowful moan in his coma. Finally, Stevie had to drag mother out of the room.

As the youngest I was the last in line to be with my father. When finally my turn arrived and I saw my gaunt dying father, I was overcome with remorse, pity, and anger. He opened his eyes, and I felt his love wash over me. I didn't want him to die without expressing my gratitude for inspiring a connection with my Indian roots and for sharing his passion for the great outdoors. I held on to his hand and spoke in sobs. "Your spirit will always walk with me in the outdoors." I bent down to kiss him, and he smiled before he slipped back into coma. "I'll always be your little brave redheaded squaw warrior," I whispered in his ear.

Ernest Ryan died quietly a few days later. That morning I awoke suddenly at 4:30 a.m. to the sound of the rustling wind outside the window. As clear as a bell I heard his voice say, "Look my little brave redheaded squaw warrior, I'm moving in the wind of peace and love. Never forget my love for you." I knew instantly that my father had died. Within five minutes the hospital called to announce that his death had occurred at 4:30 a.m.

Death was in the air. My Uncle Kenny, my dad's brother, had visited my father in the hospital a few days earlier and the following evening had suffered a major heart aneurysm before dying on the operating table. We had my Uncle Kenny's funeral, followed by my father's.

Ernie's funeral was as chaotic as his life. The triplets were in shock. They hovered by the open casket holding on to him in disbelief. Two of the triplets climbed into his coffin. It would have flipped off of its stand if not for the quick-footed funeral director who caught the coffin before Dad was tossed on the floor. Meanwhile, Mother was jockeying with Laura for the wifely right to stand in the reception line and to receive the flag draped over my father's coffin. Steve, Sandra, and I agreed that the only way to do this scene was absolutely wasted. We slipped out of the funeral parlor to a bar down the street.

My father's final resting place was in a beautiful cemetery overlooking the Hunter Mountain Ski Bowl. As we stood around his coffin I watched a stream bubbling along its path and heard beavers building their dam. My father would have company.

I was unprepared for the sense of hollowness and despair that overcame me at my father's death. He had been my first male love, and now he was gone.

The loss was unbearable. I collapsed into bed and slept. For the first time in my life, I stopped moving. After a while, I managed to drag myself out of bed to go to the job site, but once there I would sit frozen in the truck. Jacob was losing patience with me. He came stomping out to his truck one afternoon as I was having a cry.

"Christa, it's been a week since you've come back to work," he pleaded. "Are you going to do anything other than sit in the truck and cry? You need to put your mind on something other than your pain." His words solicited a flood of sobs. "Your father was a drunk," he shouted. "He wasn't worth it."

"Fuck you and your insensitivity," I flared. "It's all about the buck for you. You just don't like having to work hard for a change."

I had no coping skills and could not get back into a working rhythm. I was a catatonic mess and knew that I needed to do something. The quick fix had always been to book a trip. Jacob and I took off for Bermuda, where I continued to sob my heart out. Jacob spent the trip chasing a rare frigate bird that he had spotted ten minutes after landing on the island. I felt abandoned. I spent my time drunk and staring at a beautiful cove, watching flying fish jumping out of the water. The feelings were so devastating that I screamed at the top of my lungs:

GOD! YOU TOOK MY DADDY TOO EARLY! HE'LL NEVER BE ABLE TO TAKE MY CHILDREN FISHING! I FEEL AS THOUGH YOU'RE ROBBING ME AGAIN! THERE HAS GOT TO BE MORE

TO MY LIFE THAN ALL THIS PAIN AND SUF-
FERING! WHAT LESSON AM I SUPPOSE TO BE
LEARNING HERE?

The lesson was that my father had died from
alcoholism. Ironically, the painful experience drove
me closer to the drink.

10

Brother Can You Spare a Mansion or Two?

Life felt surreal. I was daydreaming in my truck, sitting in traffic at a stoplight in East Hampton through three light changes. It was August in the Hamptons, and no one was going anywhere soon. As I waited for the gridlock to move, I watched all the pedestrians swarming through the streets.

Since my father's death, Jacob had been emotionally missing in action. Our fights had become more violent. It was not unusual for him to issue a slap in the face or a punch in the ribs during an argument. I was learning to quiet myself when his hand was raised. I didn't want to rock the boat and convinced myself that I was to blame for causing his behavior. The feeling of intense loss at my father's passing exposed an emotional vulnerability in me that needed attention. But I was incapable of understanding my emotions. Instead, I pretended that my relationship with Jacob was normal. My denial file was filling rapidly.

I arrived at an estate that overlooked the ocean and sat in my truck listening to the roar of the surf pounding the beach and surveyed the panoramic view of the seven-acre property that included a pool and pool house, a gazebo, a large tee-pee, and a huge vegetable garden. We had nicknamed the owners *Big Bucks on the Hill.*

I looked up on the veranda and saw four masons standing with their pants down at their ankles, literally hanging in the breeze and yelling, "Yo bitch, yo girls, how 'bout it, come on, come on." *Oh my God. This is all I need!*

Their intended audience was my all-female college crew who were weeding in the vegetable garden. The girls wore next to nothing when they worked because it was so hot. "Get your pants the hell back on right now!" I screamed. I was immediately on the phone with the head contractor, threatening to press charges for indecent exposure. The head contractor was soon screeching onto the property, almost crashing into a tree. He jumped out of his truck and screamed, "All of you are fired, fired, fired!"

He canned six hands and three masons that day. "Oh, well," said one of the girls, "if only they were good-looking!"

A huge outdoor landscaping project was near

completion, and I felt proud of the work: a cascading waterfall with a swimming pool at the bottom, a brick veranda, four colorful sprawling gardens, and a pond with a bridge. Unfortunately, the inside construction had not been completed on time. There's no more forlorn family than one whose *house isn't going to be ready for the summer in the Hamptons.* Mr. and Mrs. Big Bucks had decided to be gypsies and visit Egypt and Israel for the summer.

The following week the house was finally ready for occupancy. The Big Bucks were thrilled and brought out their little girl, the housekeeper, and ten guests. The thrill didn't last long: I received a phone call from Mrs. Big Bucks, "Christa, you have got to get over here. We have an emergency!" She was beside herself. "Everything is backing up. We can't use water. We can't flush toilets. We have to shit in fear!"

Jacob and I headed for the basement. By the time we reached the fourth step, it was clear that the entire floor was covered in *you know what.* The garage was in the basement, and her little white Mercedes SL was covered in converted Filet Mignon that was dripping out of the pipes and onto the plush Italian leather seats. Brand new china in opened boxes had been shipped over from Italy was now stained brown. The glassware, still in its crates, was filling up with chocolate-colored liquid, and it wasn't mousse. I put my hand over my mouth and gagged.

"I hope you've called the plumber," I said to an ashen Mrs. Big Bucks.

"All we have to do is find out where the lid to the

septic tank is," said Jacob.

I turned to Mrs. Bucks, "Do you know where the tank is?" She was virtually catatonic. "Do you have the blueprints of the original house?" I urgently insisted. She could only roll her eyes and mutter incoherently, "Now where would they be—maybe in a file box somewhere underneath all that crap downstairs?"

We quickly called our handyman friend, Errol, who was someone who always seemed to be able to bring positive energy to lousy situations.

"Do you have an idea of where the septic might be?" he asked calmly.

"Yeah, somewhere beneath the huge ivy bed out front, between the house and the road," I suggested.

"All right, I'll be right down." Errol brought an enormous metal rod with him and began to methodically shove it through the ivy in hopes of hearing a loud clunk, which would signify the cement cover of the septic tank.

We spent our entire weekend looking for the tank cover. Needless to say, the Big Bucks and all of their guests fled back to the city.

Finally, on Monday Errol was successful. "I found the top! I found the lid!" From that point on he was "darling Errol." The septic guys came and sucked out the main tank, and then the plumber came and opened the line from the tank up to the house. It unclogged and flowed like the River Nile.

"Darling Errol" and I often ended up being on the same job site together and had become good friends.

Errol was relatively new to the East End. He had taken up kayaking and often asked me to join him. Our first adventure was unforgettable.

We left Accabonac Harbor midday and paddled toward Gardiner's Island. I was excited to be out on the water in our low, sleek Chinook-outfitted kayaks. I had chosen to believe that Errol, an experienced kayaker, had checked both the weather forecast and the tide charts.

It took longer to reach Gardiner's Island than I had anticipated. The wind had picked up and we were bucking the tide. I was tired and had cramps. We came across a dreen on the shoreline of the island and decided to paddle up to it to take a break from the roughening bay waters. I knew that going on the island was off limits, but we were technically just in the water. The dreen ended in a beautiful inland pond edged with unspoiled beaches and filled with birds.

Wow! This is incredible, God's country! We were surrounded by beauty, tranquility at its finest. Errol and I sat in our boats gazing about and taking in the aura of the island. We got out of our boats and walked along the rim of one of the beaches, when the sound of a truck and the flashing of lights suddenly interrupted the peace.

What the hell is going on here? It was the caretaker of the island. "You're under arrest! Didn't you read the signs?"

"Signs? What signs?" questioned Errol.

I could tell this guy was a real marine drill sergeant and a frustrated cowboy.

Oh my God, here we go!

"So, you're a wise guy huh? I know what to do with wise guys." He reached for his handheld radio to contact the marine police.

"Look sir, please. This is my fault." I went into the best acting I had ever done. I knew my name would be in the paper and that there was a very stiff fine of $10,000 per person if we were found trespassing on Gardiner's Island.

My legs had cramps," I pleaded. "I had no other choice. I was in bad shape."

The wind was picking up and the tides were changing direction. "Lady, I've been working the water a long time," the marine drill sergeant said, "In order to come out in that water you have to be either an experienced kayaker or out of your mind."

"He's an experienced kayaker and I'm outta my mind. I've never been kayaking before. We got lost." I continued to plead.

Errol was dying to put his two cents in, and I was stepping all over his feet. *Errol just let me handle this please. If anything, this guy can be sympathetic to a woman in need.* I went on about how we didn't know where we were and that we were lost. The winds had picked up. The tides had changed. I got cramps. I took full responsibility. And of course, I threw in a bit of sniffling.

"Well, we can handle this one of two ways. Are you experienced and capable enough to go back on the open water and head back to Accabonac Harbor, or do you want me to call marine police?" he questioned.

Oh, great, yeah. This will be a story all around town. Here I am with Errol Speed and his wife is home with the six kids.

"If you could just help us get the kayaks over this little sandbar and let me walk around to try to get rid of my cramps," I said as I was stretching and bending. I was really working it up big time with the muscle cramp thing and even threw in that I had my period.

Fortunately, the caretaker warmed up to our situation. With a sign of relief, I saw him put down his handheld radio. He helped us move the kayaks over the sandbar and into the open water on the other side of the island. The current was racing beyond anything I could paddle. Luckily, Errol threw me a rope and said, "Look, this is my fault. I'll get us out of here." I tied his line onto my boat and proceeded to paddle with whatever strength I had left. When we finally reached Accabonac Harbor, it was late afternoon and I was exhausted. I could have collapsed right then and there on the beach and died. But through it all, I was amazed how much I enjoyed kayaking.

11

Lesson #2: When in Doubt, Run, Don't Walk

By summer's end of 1985, I slowly began returning to a shadow of my normal self. What helped me along the way was discovering Kipling's Restaurant and the Kipling Players. Upon returning home one night from Jacob's radio show, we heard some beautiful music tumbling onto the street from a small bar and grill. We stopped in and listened to Jim Demitrack on guitar, Hunky Page on piano, and Ernie Furtado on bass. They were playing some very cool jazz sambas. From that night on Jacob and I made a steady diet of this jazz scene.

The late nights at Kiplings were taking their toll. The evenings would begin with Jacob and me enjoying great music, champagne and cocaine, and disintegrating into a drunken battle of wills. I would leave the nightclub before midnight, and Jacob would carry on into the night. Despite my intake, I was aware of the need to get up the next morning to meet the crew. He would find his way home in the wee hours, very drunk. This would lead to screaming arguments. He was angry over my early departure and I over his irresponsibility. While I was on the job in the early hours, he blew off his commitment and slept until noon.

Our estrangement from each other grew. Jacob found solace in his musician cronies and attending concerts. I slipped further away as I sat at home alone clutching a bottle. He was driving drunk and crashed several of our vehicles. My complaints over his drunk driving always led to an argument.

One night he came home drunk as usual. I awoke from my own inebriated slumber and asked sarcastically, "Do I still have a truck?"

"I don't know where the hell it is," he scoffed.

"You asshole!"

He snapped and grabbed my throat and started choking me until I couldn't breathe. I kicked and punched my way out of his grasp, ran off the boat, jumped into his truck, and drove like hell. I called his brother. "Come and get him or I'll call the police!" Jacob's brother convinced him to leave the boat for the night. The following morning Jacob called and woke me from a fitful sleep. He asked me to pick him up so we could talk and go to work together. I went and got him. Nothing was said and we resumed the status quo.

That night he apologized with his passion. I

was sleeping when I felt him carefully remove my nightgown. He began to touch me, arousing such heat that I was crying for him to enter me. He made love to me with a raw intensity that was overwhelming. After multiple orgasms, we collapsed in exhaustion.

The next morning a feeling of emptiness and despair began enveloping me and continued through the fall season. We had crossed a line. I ignored the violence in order to keep the booze flowing, the cock glowing, and the bank account growing.

We bought a piece of property in Springs, an affordable part of East Hampton, in March of 1986. We designed the house and had the land cleared for the builders. While our house was being built, we decided to upgrade to a larger boat so that we could be a bit more comfortable. While we were on a roll, we went all out buying two new vehicles. The debts piled up and the money making pressure was on.

To complicate matters even further, we kicked out the builders and took it upon ourselves to paint and do all the finish work. We spent the whole winter of 1986-87 working on our new house. During this winter I had my first miscarriage. I was pregnant in early December and lost the baby by mid-January.

Jacob was spending more time at the television and radio stations and less time at work. His radio show had become popular, and he was a well-known entity with our clients. It was good for business and good for his ego. The business had become old hat and he wanted to branch off. "I've been doing this for twenty-five years," he said. "I need to do something else."

I decided to branch off myself. In the fall of 1987, my mother and I opened an antique shop called The Silly Pot in Kingston. She had retired from teaching and needed to keep busy. We both loved antiques and had many adventures and great fun together. We even put on our own antique show.

During this period, we would often talk about my marriage. One day after I had a horrible fight with Jacob, she asked, "Why do you stay with him and take his abuse? At the rate you're going, someone is going to get hurt badly, and it will probably be you."

I couldn't listen to a woman I had watched endure so much in her marriage. I left the room and gravitated toward an open bottle of wine on the kitchen counter. Jeanne followed, continuing to remind me that I was repeating her legacy. I tuned her off and out!

Reality struck with the stock market crash of 1987. The big work projects of the *go-go years* stalled. The champagne and cocaine were put on hold. It was like somebody suddenly pulled the emergency brake, and we came screeching to a halt, with some of us going through the windshield.

Many of our clients had accumulated vast amounts of money by dabbling big time in the stock market, and consequently the bulk of their fortunes dwindled. No more huge jobs and installment checks awaited us. We were forced to operate on bare bones, budgeting primarily for necessities and maintenance.

In the midst of this, I got a call from the Albany Medical Center. My sister Sandra had fallen down the attic stairs at my mother's house and broken her back in three places. She was in critical condition requiring immediate open-back surgery. The alcoholic DT's complicated her recovery, and she was sedated with large doses of morphine. One night Sandra was put in a straight jacket because she was hallucinating so badly. She was in the hospital for eight weeks.

Once she was released, I packed my bags and headed up to Boston to care for her. It wasn't long after she was settled in that she began craving a drink. I discouraged her from imbibing.

We decided a bath would help her relax. After the bath water was drawn, I lowered Sandra into the tub and nearly dropped her upon site of the scars and stitches across her back and stomach. "Oh, my God!" I broke down into sobs. When I recovered, I said, "San, I don't think I can live through another tragic death. Don't you think you should slow down your drinking a little?"

"Yeah sure," she snapped, "when I get done making up for lost time from being in the hospital for eight weeks without a drop to drink."

"Sandra, please, you're scaring me."

"Christa, my drinking is my own damn business. Mind your own drinking."

Her words touched a nerve. I didn't want to think about my own escalating problems with alcohol. I was no longer just downing one bottle of wine a night, but augmenting it with a shot or two of tequila or rum. I was small in stature but my tolerance was high. My overactive metabolism burned the alcohol off quickly. For a little woman, I packed a wallop.

GOOD GOD, I'M IN A LOT OF PAIN AND CAN BARELY SORT THROUGH MY EMOTIONS. I'M BEGINNING TO THINK WE'RE ALL BROKEN AND WILL NEVER MEND.

12

Lesson #3: Forgive But Don't Forget

What I had observed through my work with the rich and famous was that money could not buy happiness or health. It couldn't keep loved ones from dying of cancer, unexpected tragedies from happening, or marriages together. Money could not solve all problems. People could try every new fad under the sun in an attempt to make themselves whole, but the end result was generally the same. No matter how big the diamond or how lovely the new clothes, materialism could not fill the emptiness that so many people experienced. This was the loud lament that echoed throughout the Hamptons. Wealth and arrogance allowed people to show a false sense of happiness, but a huge void lay underneath it all.

We worked for a couple on Lily Pond Lane, Jeanne and Jacques Escargot. They were owners of a large winery in France and part owners of a French auto company. They lived in a huge French chateau on ten acres of land in East Hampton for one month and in luxuriousness on the Riviera for the rest of the year. The Escargots would always arrive in the Hamptons on August 1st with their entourage, which included a housekeeper, a chauffeur, and two French poodles. The poodles, Mimi and Winnie, had first-class seats on the Concorde and everything just short of a split of Dom Perignon.

Mr. Escargot was probably one of the most handsome, debonair men I have ever had the pleasure of meeting. He never uttered a cross word and was a very positive person. He could always be spotted in town or at the beach peddling his little Peugeot bike or tooling around in his favorite sports car.

Mrs. Escargot, on the other hand, was a bitter demanding woman who required instant gratification. She was a cancer survivor and lived as if each day was her last. Many people who survive cancer take on a new philosophy believing that it is a gift to be alive, embracing each day as a new beginning and looking at life through unclouded eyes. Not so with Mrs. Escargot. Nothing was ever done fast enough or well enough for her. The cancer took its toll, and there were moments when she would float in and out of pure gratitude and then back to instant gratification.

It was difficult working under these conditions. What kept Jacob and me motivated was the fact that their paychecks kept us going through the winter. Each January, our fax machine spit out a complete itemized list of demands. All items over and above our contract with the Escargots were extras. What did we care? It was more money in our pockets, and it added a lot of excitement to our life. We stayed in constant contact with the secretary in the city.

Everyone who is anyone is in the Hamptons in August. Lily Pond Lane becomes "White Tent Lane" as party after party is thrown. The Escargots were planning the party of all parties that August: their daughter was getting married and twelve hundred of their "most intimate friends" were flying in from Europe. That was on top of the seven to eight hundred acquaintances who summered in the Hamptons. *I don't think their ten acres of lawn will be enough to house this extravagant production!*

By August, I am always numb from burnout, and this wedding was really pushing the limits of my patience. It was scheduled for Labor Day weekend, and we had to get the place picture perfect. This was no small feat. We traipsed all over the East End looking for plants to create pots and hanging baskets. Usually by August the Escargots' lawn is burnt out because they never went to the expense of installing an irrigation system. Consequently, we had to move sprinklers around regularly to keep the lawn green and lush. There was no question that there had to be a carpeted lawn under the wedding guests' Gucci loafers.

The weekend of the wedding arrived and everything was in tip-top shape. As I was walking the grounds Lucille, the housekeeper, began franticly waving at me to come over. She motioned for me to listen to a conversation between Mrs. Escargot and her daughter.

"I don't understand how you could have done this?" Mrs. Escargot moaned. "You've ruined my party! Your father and I have spent an enormous amount of money on this whole wedding for you. Why it occurred to you to go out and play tennis the day before your wedding, I'll never, ever understand. You've never even played tennis in your entire life. Why would you take it up now?"

"Oh, Mother, I am so sorry."

"Sorry! Sorry isn't good enough for me. Close to a million-dollar wedding plus a thirty-thousand-dollar dress and you won't even be able to walk down the aisle with your father, let alone dance with him or your new husband. You can forget about your honeymoon hiking trip in the Rocky Mountains and just stay in bed with that playboy of a husband." *Hmmm... that doesn't sound so bad. I wouldn't mind that right now, lying around with room service!*

Mrs. Escargot went on and on about the money they had spent flying their friends in, not to mention the caterers and this, that, and everything else.

Lucille was laughing hysterically.

"What's going on?" I asked.

"The bride—she broke her leg!"

"You've gotta be kidding me!"

"No, no. Take a look..."

Lucille and I moved over to the window. There

stood the bride-to-be with a full cast on her leg.

"Why the hell did you take up tennis now?" screamed her mother.

Mrs. Escargot's party was ruined. Her only daughter had brought her to one of the biggest disappointments she ever had to endure, next to her cancer, of course.

"When are we going to have children? When are we going to have children?" Jacob was a broken record. I was under constant pressure from him to start a family. There was this incredibly nagging feeling in my soul that something was not connecting, and I was uncertain about having children. I had already suffered through two miscarriages and was beginning to think that I was incapable of giving birth.

"You know, you gotta get serious," he kept hammering. "We have a lot to offer our children."

How am I going to do this?

An incredible job was offered to us on West End Road working for a movie director. I estimated the price tag of the contract was somewhere in the six-digit range and nearly hyperventilated at the anticipation of adding that to our income. But Jacob balked, saying, "I don't want to be a part of that. I know what goes on in there."

In the gardening world, it takes approximately three years for plants to reach their true fruition, from the time they are planted in the garden until the time they actually come into their mature state. Sometimes a client will be impatient and want instant perfection and flowers in bloom through the season. To accomplish this we rip up plants and rearrange them. This was one of those jobs that required us to do a lot of moving plants around like furniture.

I know we can handle that and then some.

"Christa, think about it!" Jacob implored. "How would you feel if after you got done flowering you were uprooted and disposed of so coldheartedly? This isn't an interchangeable, disposable business that we're in. We're working with life. Trees and shrubs are living life."

"I wish you were as concerned about me," I pouted."

"Christa, I'm beginning to realize that nothing in life interests you unless it has some hint of money attached to it." Ouch. His words went directly into my gut!

I knew that we were coming in highly recommended with a great chain of referrals and would most likely get the job. Jacob didn't even want to go to the interview. Then one night I heard him on the phone, turning down the project. I was flabbergasted. *How can he turn down this kind of opportunity?*

After he hung up the phone, he turned to me and said, "All I want you to concentrate on is having children."

In the late fall of 1989, another violent, drunken brawl between Jacob and me led to the neighbors calling the police. After the police left, something in me shut down. I came to the conclusion that I had to fish or cut bait. I decided to move out.

Friends of mine, Dick and Mame, owned the infamous Sea Salt Cottages in Springs. They offered me a place to crash. I planted myself in one of the cottages and continued doing business as usual with my clients, while trying to pull myself together. I got involved with a couple of spiritual support groups and spent evenings going from one charity fundraiser to another.

I was so confused. I missed the sexual life Jacob and I had together, and after surveying the open market on available single males, I was very discouraged. All I met was a bunch of cocky, egocentric men who were looking for June Cleaver.

I felt desperate and alone. Was I making a mistake leaving Jacob? The misery that our arguments had produced faded as I remembered the good times on our sailboat. The separation had given me an opportunity to see my failures in the marriage. I started to have a change of heart. *How could something that we had worked so long and so hard for be so wrong?*

After four months, I moved back home.

13

From Cradle to Garden

All my friends were settling down and starting families. Perhaps there was something to this "baby thing" that Jacob had been pushing for so hard. Maybe having a child would solve some of our issues. If the problems in my marriage did stem from my reluctance to have a family, it was temporarily resolved when I got pregnant in April. I miscarried again at the end of June.

This was my third miscarriage in two years. What was going on? I started to look for a different gynecologist than the group I had used in Southampton. I had nicknamed this group "Forty Fingers" because it consisted of a group of four doctors who worked in a circle. On any given day you'd go in for an appointment and never knew which of the four doctors you'd end up seeing.

A doctor who had broken off from this group several years ago, Dr. Phil School, came highly recommended to me. I decided to meet with him. I was going to have a child. I was determined.

Dr. School had me back and forth for blood and hormone testing, and I was soon surprised to find out that I was pregnant again. I hadn't been trying because I was too scared to death to face another lost baby. I was shocked, to say the least, when the doctor told me the news. "It seems you usually lose the baby between the eighth and tenth week," he said. "That's the time your body kicks in a certain amount of progesterone. Let's put you on some progesterone and see how that works."

I kept working but not as hard. We decided to turn down a big account that was offered to us. This was disappointing, but I realized that I had enough on my plate between being pregnant and keeping up with Jacob's radio, television, and consultation schedule.

There was a heartbeat after eight weeks and the doctor gave me the thumbs up that it looked good. Fortunately, the pregnancy went well. I felt remarkably good and had no problem giving up alcohol. Jacob was thrilled, and it seemed that the pregnancy had changed his attitude towards me. Our nightlife in restaurants and clubs was put on the shelf for the time being. We did some serious open-water sailing that summer and would spend long evenings over games of chess. I was getting bigger and bigger, and it looked like this baby was going to stick around. But I still had my countless, silent doubts.

On April 30, 1991, a rainy Tuesday, I went to see Dr. Phil School. I was about two and a half weeks late at this point. He took one look at my due date and said, "I don't like this." He had me check into the hospital immediately. "Whoa, that's scary," he said. "I'm coming up with a twenty-three-and-a-half-inch-circumference chest size and a sixteen-and-a-half-inch head size. I know you stretch, but boy, you're awfully small. I don't know how much more you can expand."

I was starting to worry. Dr. School said, "You're carrying anywhere from a ten to a thirteen pound child. The kid is only going to get bigger. What do you want to do?" he asked.

"This is the 1990's," I said "I think I'll go with science."

"Good. I have a 3:30 opening this afternoon."

So I called Jacob.

"It's your life. I can't make the decision," Jacob equivocated.

"No, it's *our* life, I'm carrying *our* child," I fired back. He hemmed and hawed, clearly wanting no accountability in the decision. I decided to have the C-section. I asked to be sedated and knocked out before going into the delivery room, and asked Jacob to stay close by. Then in I went.

I wasn't nearly as graceful coming out. I had excruciating pain railing through my entire body. I was heavily sedated when they wheeled me up to the room. I'll never forget Jacob sitting in the chair, talking to this perfect little baby and asking me, "How are you feeling?"

"Like a truck ran over me and then proceeded to back up and run over me again," I replied.

He brought me our son, who he wanted to name after himself. I kept remembering something my grandmother Roberts had always said, "You want to give your child a name that's going to make him stand out." I wanted something really grand, something that would honor my grandmother, so I decided that I would like to name our son after her.

After three days in the hospital, we finally agreed on a name: Robert Christopher Durite. He was a ten-pound, red-haired, beautiful, smiling child.

"Yeah, he's been smiling since he came out," Jacob said.

"Isn't that a sign of gas?" I replied.

But this was not gas; it was Robert's disposition. He had the sunniest, most easygoing nature. Best of all, he slept through the night. Being the mother of this child was a total blessing. This little bundle brought me so much love, peace, and enjoyment that I was completely awed with my newfound job.

Jacob was very patient and loving. Fatherhood was beyond his expectations. Robert's good nature delighted us to no end. My new role as a mother created moments of pure joy and an awareness of love that I had never before experienced. I was starting to feel that God might not have abandoned me.

I was able to get back to work unusually fast for a new mother. At times, Robert would be tossed into the truck with me with all of the baby paraphernalia and off we'd go. I was with my baby, enjoying being back to work like I had never left. The beat rolled on. *Oh my gosh! This is so easy.*

Jacob and I decided we would look into getting a bigger house. Our two-bedroom cottage didn't look so big when you added all the toys and paraphernalia. We found a comparative "mini mansion" across from the Grace Estate, four hundred acres of state preserve filled with beautiful Lodgepole pines. We were about a mile from the beach and had four weekenders and one year-rounder living on our road at the time. The house was an adorable 3500-square-foot colonial set back on three acres. It was a birdwatcher's dream come true. *Oh, my God. We'll never grow into this.*

Life was busy between taking care of Robert, moving into our new home, and keeping the business running smoothly. Time passed quickly, and because I was so busy and so enthralled at being a mother, I overlooked Jacob slipping back into his old habits. Coming home from his Sunday night radio show, he began stopping off at the bar at Kiplings, staying out later, and drinking more. He had also met up with some of his old cronies and started playing with a band again.

My new parental mindset opened my eyes to a lot of things about Jacob that were very difficult to face and accept. I tried broaching the subject that I could use more support in the business and with the domestic responsibilities. He did not react well to my implication that our relationship was becoming unbalanced due to the amount of time he spent away from home. No matter how hard I tried, it just didn't seem like I could get through to him.

How much of this was worth fighting for? I was happy in my new home. I had my baby and enough money…

I didn't want to face any more arguments. It was much easier to be compliant; compliance felt like an old comfortable slipper. So I put on the slipper and continued my descent into a serious state of denial.

14

Stormy Weather

The next few years I spent struggling with nannies for Robert. I had heard my share of *nanny nightmare stories*. Fortunately, my nanny nightmare days came to an end when I was introduced to Nanny Coy. She was a gentle southern woman in her early fifties who had just finished successfully raising four of her own children. She had a great outlook on life and loved kids. She was capable, willing, and best of all, available. Robert was immediately comfortable with Nanny Coy, and my childcare issue was resolved.

The next two years rolled by quickly. Between the help I got from Nanny Coy and the support I got from my other new-mother friends, my life was running smoothly. Robert was three when I found out I was pregnant again. And unlike my first pregnancy, I truly embraced the idea without all the doubts. Robert was thrilled at the idea of having a new brother or sister. We spent many an hour decorating the nursery together and preparing for the new arrival. There was no apprehension on his part. He was so excited!

Unfortunately, I began noticing a dramatic change in Jacob's routine. He was struggling to balance his workdays with his nighttime activities. The days started later and the nights lasted longer. I was alone more often. All-night partying was not conducive to raising a family and running a successful business. I had stopped drinking when I became pregnant and was beginning to see things as I had never seen them before. It was making me anxious. With two children and huge financial obligations, I was feeling trapped in my marriage.

One October morning in my ninth month, I awoke with a deep feeling of loneliness and sorrow welling up inside of me, seemingly out of nowhere. By nine o'clock that morning I was not feeling any movement from the baby. I started to tap at my stomach. *"Wake up!"* I wanted to do my favorite bonding activity, which involved putting on music, dancing, and feeling the baby's spirit and feet kicking to the music in time.

As the day moved on, I became more fearful, with a deep sense that something was drastically wrong. I called up Dr. Phil School and cried over the phone. He was sweet and comforting and told me to come in immediately for a sonogram. The sonogram confirmed that there was no heartbeat, no movement. I sobbed my heart out. It never occurred to me that this could happen. I was nine months pregnant! I was hysterical. Dr. School muttered, "We'll have to induce you." I don't remember driving home from the doctor's office. I broke the news to Jacob. He told me that I should get another sonogram and a second opinion. I could see in his eyes that none of what I told him was sinking in. He was in denial.

Jacob and I went in the next day. They induced me and out came a little redheaded girl with amazingly blue eyes and thick, long, black eyelashes. She was beautiful. But she was dead, just dead. While I delivered the baby Jacob sat with me and wept, but he refused to look at her. When the nurse pressed him to view her, he left the room.

"Here's your baby, honey," the nurse said as she put the baby in my arms. "Hold her for a little while longer. You have to say your goodbyes."

I took my daughter, who I had named Christine, and held her in my arms for a long time. I was waiting for her to wake up and come back to life. I hadn't cried yet, but I knew the flood was near. I was all alone, which pushed me further into depression. A piece of me died along with my baby. The nurse took her away from me after two hours and gave me drugs to sleep.

Jacob was lost in silent grief. He couldn't tolerate the pain and went to great lengths to distance himself from his grief. He was unable to talk to me about anything concerning our baby. I wanted him to hold me. If we could cry in each other's arms and comfort one another, it might provide an opportunity to heal together. But he was incapable of letting me in, and we both suffered through our heartbreak desperately alone.

The following day on my way home, my eyes were opened and I moved, but I felt lifeless. I couldn't think. I simply sat on the couch and stared at the wall, day after day. I was in a profound bereavement, overcome with waves of anger, self-hatred, remorse and denial, all of the benchmarks of a person living through grief.

Several months earlier, Jacob and I had made plans for a week's vacation on an island off the coast of Virgin Gorda in the British Virgin Islands. We had rented a place right on the water. I sobbed my eyes out from the time we got on the plane through the entire vacation. I mixed a steady diet of booze and sleeping pills, ignoring the vision that kept flashing in my head of my mother passed out on the bathroom floor.

After we returned from the islands, I was still unable to cope, and Jacob became weary with me quickly. Our anger was unmanageable and would rise to the surface in an instant. After one horrendous argument, I was despondent. I looked at my tear-streaked face in the bathroom medicine cabinet as though it belonged to a stranger. I watched myself reach into the cabinet for the bottle of Valium, screw off the top, and empty the contents into my palm. I put the pills into my mouth two at a time and swallowed them with a glass of wine, then brushed my hair, washed my face, and lay down on top of my bed.

The next thing I remember was my four-year-old son trying to wake me from a deep sleep. I dragged myself out of the bed and went into the bathroom, forcing myself to vomit up the pills. I was horrified by what I had almost done. Only my love for Robert gave me the will to live. I would not have my child grow up carrying the burden of his mother's suicide.

Jacob and I went for counseling. He was furious at my inability to recover. I sat on the therapist's couch and cried through the hour appointment. The therapist tried to help us hear one another with more compassion, but there was too much static to penetrate. After a few sessions, we stopped going. The situation between us continued to deteriorate.

The problems were compounded by my inability to work. Our income plunged. Fear and uncertainty engulfed my every waking and sleeping hour. I would take hour-long walks everyday and have rage attacks directed at God.

ARE YOU LISTENING? I HAVE EXPERIENCED PROFOUND PAIN, BUT THIS IS UNBEARABLE! MY GOD IN HEAVEN, HAVE YOU NO HEART? I HATE YOU FOR DOING THIS TO ME!

In an attempt to use the anger constructively, I began writing a book about my experience. Through talking with other women, discovering the commonality of pain, and by putting pen to paper, I developed some coping skills. I wrote *From the Depths of a Woman's Soul* about what happens to people, mainly women, but also couples, when they lose a child. Some women never return to fully function in society and a large percent of the couples end up in divorce. These were some very scary statistics that I took seriously.

My mother came to visit and I gave her a copy of the book to read. I could hear her sobbing uncontrollably in the guest room. I went to her and we sat on the bed holding one another and crying together. After exhausting ourselves she spoke, "As difficult as my life has been, I cannot conceive of the idea of losing a child. You are a very courageous woman."

Just like that, my pain was validated. For months Jacob had accused me of being self-centered and over-emotional. I didn't understand the pain of my loss and felt shame at my prolonged suffering. My mother assured me that I deserved the right to grieve and needed to give myself enough time to go through the process. That initiated a shift in my acceptance of the pain and a desire to seek a deeper level of understanding.

I poured through spiritual books and began writing a journal. I was searching for myself. All of my life I had lived in yesterday and tomorrow, never today. Tomorrow might not come. It didn't come for my daughter, and her death taught me that I had to learn how to live in the now. I was taking for granted the wonderful gift in front of me, my very much alive son, Robert. I spent as much time as possible with this sweet child, and through my gratitude for him, began to see the light shining through again.

3

My *Life* Was Officially Out of *Control*

The only truths that count
are truths that mature slowly.
~ Erik Orsenna on Andre Le Notre

15

Distractions in the Key of E-Minor

April 23, 2004

I have finally managed to scrape together a year of this thing called sobriety. I celebrated my first anniversary at an AA meeting this evening and then went for coffee afterwards with a group of friends. I am feeling elated over my accomplishment and hopeful that the future will be better than the past. The spiritual lift I have been experiencing in the program is teaching me to believe in gratitude and forgiveness. In my heart I still truly love Jacob and I have faith that our life is going to turn around.

I pull into the driveway and hear loud music. It's a tape of Jacob's god-forsaken band that has never amounted to much. The ear-splitting decibels do not bode well. My stomach twists into knots as I open the door.

"Where the fuck have you been?" The alcoholic fumes coming toward me speak volumes. He's drunk. "You're fucking someone, you dumb stupid fucking bitch!" he screams.

"I went to an AA meeting," I plead.

He raises his hand to slap me, but I am quicker than he is and duck the blow.

Damn it! What have I done to make him so angry? Was I gone too long? Where are the children?

He grabs me by the hair and pins me to a chair. SMACK! This time he connects, leaving me dazed.

"When are you going to get your shit together?" He turns dismissively and leaves the room.

I shouldn't have gone to my anniversary. Fuck! What am I thinking? I worked my ass off for my year. Why am I blaming myself? He's a violent drunk. When am I going to stop allowing him to abuse me?

1995

Whatever our problems, sex was not one of them. Jacob and I had just completed a very satisfying session of lovemaking; one that I was almost positive had conceived another child. I had lured him into the bedroom a half hour earlier, assuring him that it was a safe time and contraceptives were not needed. It was my secret. Jacob was adamantly against having another child, so I tricked him. I was determined to become a mother again. A month later I was thrilled when it was confirmed that I was pregnant.

"How did you fuck this up?" Jacob ridiculed.

"I want a child."

"You and your childbearing desires. You're reckless."

I didn't care what he thought. I found a wonderful doctor in Riverhead, and given my difficult pregnancies, tried to put my fears on hold. Intuitively, I believed the child was a boy. By my February checkup, the doctor declared that the baby was breech and the umbilical cord wrapped around his neck. A week later a decision was made to take the baby three weeks early.

Later that day, I gave birth to a seven-pound, six-ounce curly red-haired blue-eyed beautiful baby boy. After the initial shock, Jacob had come to accept my pregnancy, and we were both happy to name our son Richard.

Spring started late that year, giving me a little more time to recover with the new baby before it was necessary to address the business. I didn't know how I was going to coordinate taking care of two children, the housework, and resume my previous work schedule. I could feel Jacob watching me to see when I was going to spring into action. He was looking for relief from the day-to-day obligations of the business. But I was exhausted and didn't want to be rushed back to work.

"The business needs somebody full-time and it can't be me," I shouted in frustration as he walked out the door to go bird watching. We could no longer afford the luxury of Jacob spending most of his time on pretty much anything but the business. Too much of the responsibility of home life and work life had been on my shoulders.

It had been seventeen years since Jacob and I had gotten together. Over that time, he had been a frustrated artist who never quite fulfilled his promise. As the dream drew further away, his anger and self-hatred grew. After striking out as a musician, his last strong connection to the world he loved was his radio show. His nightspot on WLIU kept alive Jacob's illusion that he was more than a landscaper. The show's popularity served both of his worlds because the clients enjoyed his hip notoriety.

It all came to a crashing halt when Jacob lost his radio show because of his drinking and drugging during the broadcast. He was asked to clean up if he wanted to get back on the air, but he refused. There was no hiding the fact that he was a disappointment in both our eyes. Jacob became depressed and began drinking more, often passing out in his truck on the side of the road. When home, he was surly and hibernated in the basement. The slightest wrong move would set him off.

Jacob hated his life, and I was the target of his anger. Every conversation led to an escalated, knockdown, drag-out fight, usually over money and the dip in income because of my time off. We had never had an easy relationship, but now the pressure of family life intensified the resentments. It was war. Our arguments were hauntingly familiar, creating a feeling of agitated déjà vous from my childhood memory file. Nevertheless, I would ferociously engage in these battles, until Jacob's hand rose up, and then I'd retract like a coiled snake and slither away.

Relief only came when I gave myself permission to open a bottle of wine every afternoon at four o'clock. Those glasses of wine continued late into the evening hours.

I succumbed to the pressure and went back to work. In my first week back on the job, I had been on the job site with my female crew since 7:00 in the morning when Jacob rolled in at noon with music blasting out of his truck and the smell of pot wafting from the window. He approached the girls who were planting annuals. "Christa!" Jacob shouted commandingly. "May I see you for a moment?" I cringed at the sound of his voice.

"Luvy, why do you continuously do things ass backwards?" he asked right in front of the crew.

"Please don't speak to me like that," I said and walked away.

He followed me and chastised, "We agreed that you wouldn't rush the work and do a lousy job again!

"How dare you undermine me in front of the girls?" I confronted him. "That's over the line. I don't have to answer to you. Who the hell are you!"

"I'll tell you who I am," he shouted with an authoritative blast. "I'm the person who runs the show around here. It's my money, my business, and you answer to me. When I ask you what's happening, you tell me."

"It might be your business, but I am the one

who does the work." I turned and headed for my car, amidst shouts from Jacob.

"Come back here you dumb, stupid, fucking bitch, or there will be hell to pay."

He was still shouting as I pulled away. Fortunately, when I arrived home the house was empty. It was 1:00 p.m. as I uncorked a bottle of Merlot. "The only friend in my miserable life is booze," I thought.

A bottle of wine later, I opened a letter from a good friend and found pictures from a recent party that added insult to injury. There was a photo of me sitting by the pool in my bathing suit that I barely recognized. I was fat. I got on the scale and it rocked 158! The day I left the hospital with Richard I had weighed 115 pounds. I had gained 43 pounds.

My life was officially out of control.

In the summer of 1999, I was determined to do something about my health and appearance. I taped the picture to the kitchen cabinet so that I had to look at it before I reached for the cookies. *This can't be me.*

I found myself tired all of the time, no longer the energizer bunny. I started to look into intestinal cleanses and attempted to stop drinking. I managed to white knuckle my way through the summer and fall, but it was unexpectedly difficult.

By Thanksgiving, I had lost the weight and celebrated with a new hairdo (cutting off my trademark waist-length red hair), a new wardrobe, and a membership to a health club. For my birthday I bought myself a bike and started riding for an hour every morning. I had my old energy back. My confidence was on the upswing.

"Where the hell do you think you're going in that ridiculous outfit?" Jacob's inquiry stopped me in my tracks as I was headed out the door for a lunch date. "What's wrong with my outfit?" I asked, suddenly feeling insecure as I studied my reflection in the hallway mirror. "It would be fine if you were a sixteen-year-old girl, but you're a middle-aged woman, Christa. You've lost too much weight. You look unhealthy."

I knew Jacob was feeling threatened by my new slimness, but it didn't matter. My confidence of a few minutes earlier took a dive.

There were nasty interrogations each time I attempted to leave the house. Where was I going? Who was I meeting? When would I be home? He was having less and less of a role in my daily activities and he didn't like that.

We obtained a second mortgage, and suddenly our money problems were cleared up for the moment. Money bought the denial that shielded me from the truth that was getting difficult to ignore. Given my early poverty, financial security was the cure-all for life's problems. We were in the money again and sobriety went on the shelf. Once again, we were sailing, eating, and drinking the nights away.

16

Is That a Light at the End of the Tunnel, or a Freight Train?

It was June, our most stressful month, and business was at high mass. I came home after a day of supervising installations, running crews, and dealing with kids. I put the groceries away and opened a pint bottle of Tequila that was in the kitchen cabinet. I collapsed on the couch and surveyed the mess in the living room, too tired to clean. I turned on Oprah, and before long the bottle of Tequila was gone.

Thoroughly medicated, I didn't hear Jacob's truck pull into the driveway. I was startled when I discovered him standing over me. He reached down and shook me. "This place is a god-damned mess!

What do you do all day?"

"Why do you always come home and belittle me? Why can't you be a good husband for once?

"You're not worth it," he snarled. "You're all over the place. If I don't keep a handle on you, you lose your focus. Get up off of your ass and do something useful."

He picked me up by my sweater and pushed me against a wall. I lost it. The combination of anger and alcohol pushed me over the edge. I grabbed the empty Tequila bottle and hurled it at his head. He was stunned. This was the first time I had fought back. I picked up a folding chair and threw it at him, screaming, "No more!" This unleashed his fury, and he chased me around the house. After being cornered in the kitchen, I picked up a knife and it frightened me because in my heart I wanted to kill him. He grabbed my arm and wrenched the knife from my grip, before throwing me to the floor. I kicked and screamed, until he gave me a shot in the face that produced a white flash. He hit me again in the stomach. I managed to role over to protect myself when he kicked me in my backside. I crawled out of range, getting to my feet.

"I'm not scared of you. Fuck you!"

Before he could strike another blow, the doorbell rang. Jacob answered as I went into the kitchen and poured a glass of wine. After he got rid of whoever was at the door, I came out of the kitchen and said, "This shit has to stop!" He flashed red and with menacing tones replied, "If you know what's good for you, you'll take your ass to your room, right now!" The look in his face was frightening and my resolve weakened.

I headed upstairs and heard him drive away in his truck.

Two hours later I awoke in my bedroom to the sound of the shower running. Jacob was back. I got up and went down to the kitchen. A few minutes later he came in to get a beer. He took me by the hand and led me upstairs to the bedroom for our customary make-up sex. It was all we had left of our relationship. I felt remorse from my abhorrent behavior, and trauma bonding with Jacob provided momentary relief.

The next morning we were considerate of one another. Our light and easy communication enabled us to sweep the previous night's horror show under the rug.

In 2000, Jacob and I finally gave up trying to work together, hoping that it might reduce the stress in our relationship. The business was filed under his sole proprietorship, so technically he was the boss. He held that technicality over my head, which gave him the edge in our partnership. I wanted my independence.

There were two parts to our business: installations and maintenance. I took the installation side and he the maintenance. Installations depended upon new referrals so I was flying without a net, on my own for the first time, and it was daunting.

"You'll never make it on your own," Jacob harangued. My confidence was shaky but I pushed forward anyway. Failure was not an option.

The answer to my prayers arrived when I was hired by an extraordinary woman whose thick Brooklyn accent was at odds with her business acumen as the owner of an upscale East Hampton boutique. Candy, an attractive woman in her late fifties, became a very important client. She single-handedly pulled my start-up effort out of serious financial trouble by providing lots of work and many good referrals. Candy was a valuable mentor and friend.

One referral was as a consultant to a couple in North Sea who was buying a new house in South-ampton that was under construction. The landscapers they had hired had not yet begun work. I suggested to the couple that they reconsider the proposed location of the driveway and showed them where I thought it should be.

Two weeks later, I drove by the house, and to my astonishment, the new driveway was located where I had suggested. *Wow, somebody listened to me!* Generally, a woman's opinion on any matters that involved "heavy equipment" was considered to have less merit. It thrilled me that my idea was not only taken seriously but also actually implemented. This could never have happened with Jacob second-guessing my ideas.

That June, I was shocked to receive a phone call from the North Sea couple. They were investing in a large parcel of land and offered me the job of designing the landscape for a new home. *You have to be crazy to consider taking on a huge new project in the middle of June.* Dot Carter had been bugging me to do something to celebrate the twenty-fifth anniversary of our friendship. I told her that what I wanted was help with this big project—not exactly what she'd had in mind as a celebration, but she agreed. We jumped in full force together and worked our tails off.

I now needed to find a reliable contractor and stumbled upon Jeff from Southampton Landscaping. I showed Jeff all of the things that I had cooking and was pleased when he had an estimate for each job within a week. Usually, it takes two weeks for a contractor to return a phone call. Jeff gave me a cell phone number and the easy access was a blessing.

Jacob observed that my end of the business was prospering with little comment. My fear of falling on my face was beginning to diminish. I was finding my stride. I was making money. It felt like a new beginning.

Meanwhile, as I delivered larger and larger checks into his hands, Jacob wasn't doing very well. Without me, he was discovering that bird watching and real work didn't mix. He was late for everything: client meetings, deliveries, and supervising workers. Jacob didn't have the discipline and was falling on his ass. If he was starting to gain perspective, he didn't show it. Instead of giving me respect, he turned up the harassment.

"I don't care what you make; it's not enough. You've let our home go to hell. This isn't working! Can't you do anything right?"

Jacob's opinion became less important as my confidence grew. The rewards of pleased clients and agreeable workers were very satisfying. He couldn't complain about my work, so he wore me down in other ways, arousing guilt over my having abandoned the family's needs. That was bullshit. What he really wanted was for me to go back to the way things used to be.

I gave in and began overseeing his side of the business. It was insane for me to do it, but I thought that if Jacob could get back to his old lifestyle, he would treat me better. No matter how hard I pushed myself, he pushed me harder. I was taking care of the children, maintaining the house, keeping the business going, and staying on top of the bills, and the pressure of it all drove me toward the bottle. I was drowning in an excessive amount of alcohol. GOD, PLEASE BRING ME SOMETHING THAT WILL CHANGE MY LIFE!

One afternoon in early spring of 2001 I was at Candy's boutique when I exchanged a few pleasantries with a handsome, Armenian man in his early forties. His melodic accent lingered with me for the rest of the day. Weeks later, Candy gave me his business card and said, "His name is Jonathan and he's looking for a landscaper. I recommended you highly and he's on the hook. Go get him."

I met Jonathan on a beautiful day at his estate on the bay in North Haven. There was something exceptionally charismatic about Jonathan. His curly black hair, gorgeous smile, and deep dark eyes were spellbinding. He spoke with genuine honesty, a rarity in my world. We casually walked around the property as Jonathon described the type of landscaping he had envisioned.

We entered the house, and there was a small blaze in the fireplace and the music of Stan Getz filling the room. I looked out of an enormous picture window that overlooked the body of water between North Haven and Shelter Island. There was a beautiful sailboat anchored to a dock.

Jonathan offered me a cup of coffee, and we talked for a long time about sailing, children, and our work. As a professional photographer he had envisioned the perennial garden he wanted for his property—unstructured, colorful, magical, and changing.

"Like life itself," I suggested.

"Yes," he mused. "I want the garden to be like life, always changing, happy, bright, sad, and inspirational."

Oh my God, this man is very attractive!

"Do you ever ski?" he asked, abruptly changing the conversation.

I pictured us holding hands on a mountaintop, and then racing each other down the slopes to an awaiting warm cabin. I averted my gaze for fear that he might read my mind.

"Skiing is one of my great passions," I answered, and his face lit up.

The one thing that I always prided myself on was that I had never even entertained the idea of adultery in my twenty-three years of marriage. But out of the blue, I was having feelings that had long been buried. This man had found the dial on my meter, and it was pointing to the *yes* button with an urgency that shocked me

"My ex-wife didn't ski," he confided. "She would

sit in the lodge and drink. She had a very serious drinking problem and refused to get help."

I got a chill.

"My husband drinks," I consoled. "It's created terrible problems."

"It's hard for me to understand," he mused. "No one in my family has ever drunk more than at the occasional social function."

It was four-thirty in the afternoon, and I was just dying, dying for a glass of wine!

As I gathered my things to leave, Jonathan asked me to pull together some ideas, and I promised to call him with an estimate as soon as possible.

I forced myself to wait a week before calling. My mind was racing, creating scenarios of Jonathan and me falling in passionate love. When I heard his rich sophisticated voice at the other end of the phone, I had a quick premonition that I was headed for trouble. As always, I pushed that inner voice away.

"Jonathon, I have the plans and your estimate."

He listened intently as I laid out my design and the expected cost.

"Christa," he said when I finished my presentation, "I love your ideas and the estimate is very reasonable. I can't tell you how difficult it has been to find professional integrity. Money seems to be the be-all, end-all of existence. The Hamptons is a place of lost individuals, and I have been subjected to all kinds of lying, cheating, and disappointment. But you, my dear, are a breath of fresh air."

Jonathon was soon leaving the country for a

photo shoot in Southeast Asia and would be back in early spring. "I want to work with you," he concluded enthusiastically. "You'll hear from me no later than early May. So long, my breath of spring."

He wants me!!

17

It's Not the End of the World But I Can See the Edge

One day the kids and I stopped for a lobster salad. After eating I started to feel as if something wasn't quite right with my system. At home that night, I didn't know if I was coming or going and was in excruciating pain. I took my temperature and it had climbed past 102 degrees and continued to rise.

I was avoiding the hospital, but by the next day it felt like something was exploding inside of me. I asked Jacob to drive me to the hospital, but he didn't take me seriously. After pleading with him, I dialed 911. He acquiesced, realizing that I was almost *dead* serious.

A half hour later I lay on a stretcher in South-ampton Hospital as a handsome male nurse took my blood pressure. I leaned over, grabbed him by the throat, and shrieked, "If you value your life, get me some painkillers and a resident surgeon now!" That got his attention, and minutes later a surgeon came into the room and touched me around the appendix. I screamed so loud he backed away. The doctor quickly ordered an operating room for an emergency appendectomy.

My husband fled the hospital. Anatomy and physi-ology were not his strong suit. But his desertion left me feeling hollow and disheartened. As they wheeled me into the OR, my cell phone rang. "I want you to get dressed," he ordered through my morphine haze. "I'm coming for you. We're going to get a second opinion."

You're astonishing! Where am going to find ten men in a hurry to dress me? "Better get out the rosary beads, Jacob. I'm in trouble. This thing is about to blow." I hung up the phone.

I watched the overhead fluorescent lights dance on the OR ceiling as the anesthesiologist prepared to put me under. I felt myself floating upward into another state of consciousness. There was a profound detachment from my body that lay on the stretcher below being poked and prodded by a team of medical people. A beautiful eight-year-old girl met me. We embraced and I understood immediately that she was my daughter Christine.

"You can't die now," she said. "You've got too much life ahead of you. I love you, and I'll always be here for you when you need me."

I gained consciousness in a room with a ninety-six-year-old woman, and every night she awoke wailing and thrashing. By the fourth night I was exhausted. "I can't get any rest," I said to my doctor, "and I have to get back to work."

The doctor knew the likes of my kind. "As soon as you're released," he warned, "you'll resume the same frantic work pace and will end up back here within days." He explained that a relapse would put me in intensive care and it would take four times as long to recover. But after four days of my persistent whining, he acquiesced. That was a mistake. I was soon back in the hospital and knocked off my feet for nine weeks.

"You're going to ruin the season with this damn operation," Jacob complained. His dissatisfaction with my condition was endless. I went to the doctor when my weight dropped to ninety pounds and my hair began to fall out in chunks. He told me that my blood pressure was off the charts, my thyroid was not functioning properly, and my adrenal glands had collapsed. I was a mess. To add insult to injury, I had acquired a new addiction, Vicodin.

By early summer I had almost convinced myself that my crush on Jonathan had passed when my caller ID flashed his name, and my heart skipped several beats. He was back from Southeast Asia and wanted to meet with me to review my proposal.

Jonathan had an artistic sensibility and was not interested in the standard landscaping design. Our relationship was going to be a creative collaboration, and I was pumped to do my very best. I took him on a tour of my clients' gardens. When he liked something he saw, Jonathan would become excited and hold my arm seductively.

"Christa, it is sooooo magnificco and wonderful; you are genius and an artist!" I was captivated by his sexy accent and irrepressible smile. This was slippery ground, even if I had landscaped it myself.

As our friendship grew Jonathan became my safe haven. He was thrilled with the work on the garden and lawn and retained me to supervise the installation of the driveway. We would sit on his dock most mornings drinking coffee and talking, and I would often catch him looking at me in a curious way.

"You are very beautiful, Christa," he would say. I was never at ease with compliments and would do my best to deflect them. He noticed my moods and observed how my designs fluctuated according to my frame of mind.

"See over here," he'd say, "that was last Tuesday. You were blue and sad, weren't you? And over here— this is today. You're pink and beautiful and alive and vivacious! Over here is red, your danger zone."

I felt sure he was flirting. It made me feel more alive than I had in years and also aware of my loneliness.

Please fall in love with me!

Thoughts of Jonathan had overtaken my consciousness. I would rush appointments and blow through stop signs in order to get to his house at the end of the day, *casually* dropping by to check the progress of the driveway. I would have erotic dreams of us making love. At night I would awaken in a cold sweat and need a glass of red wine to quiet my longing enough to sleep. GOD, HOW CAN I LIVE THIS LIE!!

"The house is filthy. You're cooking sucks. You don't spend enough time with the kids." As usual there was no pleasing Jacob. Our relationship had been poisoned for so long that neither of us were capable of expressions of kindness, gentleness, or love. He had been my husband now for twenty-two years. How much longer could we do this?

It was a beautiful summer day, and I was planning a trip to the beach with my children and a young boy by the name of Adam who had a genetic DNA disorder. We had a close relationship, and I would take him on occasional outings. I was making sandwiches as Adam and Robert waited patiently at the counter. Jacob came into the kitchen with an edge on. He slammed a cup onto the counter, filled it with tea, and began stirring loudly. I felt intimidated and tried to ignore him.

"How long are you going to be at the beach?" he questioned.

"Jacob, please, don't start," I responded.

"What about that check?"

"The kids have been counting on this trip all week. I'll pick it up tomorrow."

"Where's my lunch?" he asked.

I handed him a lunchbox, and he opened it to check the contents. Suddenly, he had a wild look in his eye that could only mean trouble.

"God damn it! You dumb stupid fucking bitch!" he screamed. "How many times do I have to explain how I like my sandwich? You put too much fucking mayonnaise on it!"

He fired off an angry litany of my shortcomings. I turned toward the children, and while Robert was taking in the scene calmly, Adam looked very frightened and began to cry.

"Please, Mrs. Durite, make him stop; he's scaring me."

I approached Adam and wrapped him in my arms.

"Stop!" I screamed at Jacob. "Look what you've done."

"Serves you right, bitch, for being so negligent!" he fired back.

I led the terrified child outside, and we sat by the pool until Jacob left. Something penetrated my denial. My excuses for abusive behavior had worn completely thin. Chaos was normal for my children, but Adam's reaction demonstrated how dysfunctional we truly were.

I was sinking into desperation with an intensity that made thoughts of suicide a daily occurrence. I didn't have the guts to confront Jacob about my unhappiness or the courage to leave him, unless there was a savior to protect me.

Please Jonathan, rescue me from this life!

One evening I opened a discussion with Jacob about our collective anger and excessive drinking, but he wasn't having any of it. "We're in the heat of the season and stressed out," he said. "We don't drink any more than most people. The alcohol helps. Don't create problems, Christa." I dropped the subject as he poured me a glass of wine, but in my heart I knew that I was right. No amount of wine was able to smother that truth.

It all came to a head one horrific summer weekend when the kids were away at camp. I was in my office writing when Jacob came home. The night was hot and he seemed aggravated. "Why don't you go take a dip in the pool?" I suggested.

"I don't need a dip in the pool," he snapped. "It's Friday night. We need to get this house together."

"Uh, oh," I thought. I left the office, hoping to quell the trouble I sensed. "Its okay, Jacob. I've got all day tomorrow."

He shot me a dangerous glare and went into the bedroom. "You dumb, stupid, fucking bitch!" he roared minutes later. "The god damned sheets are wet! What the hell have you been doing all day?"

"I work a hell of a lot harder than you ever do," I fired angrily.

I immediately reproached myself for losing my temper, but it was too late. His hand flew across my face in a violent thrust that rocked my jaw. I fell on the floor and lay there as Jacob walked away dismissively. I'd had enough. I went into my bedroom and dialed 911.

Ten minutes later a police car pulled into the driveway. When I answered the door, there stood two police officers. I knew one of them; he was the uncle of Adam, the little boy who had been so frightened of Jacob. I invited them inside and quickly told them the story. The policeman recalled the story he had heard from Adam's parents, and when Jacob came into the room he confronted him sharply, telling him to leave the premises. Jacob was shocked, but did as he was told and quietly left. The policemen promised to keep an eye on the house.

Late that night, Jacob snuck back into the house and slept in the guest room. The next morning we pretended that nothing had happened. But something had happened. I felt a glimmer of self-worth for having taken a stand.

I could no longer deny the truth: our relationship was simmering in violence. I had become my mother, a battered wife. Over the years I had suffered many black eyes, several bruised ribs, and arms ripped out of sockets so often that eventually I learned how to put them back in place. Yet my denial had been rock solid.

I was sick and tired of being scared out of my skin all the time. Nothing was ever going to change in my life, until I figured out that it was me who had to change. I was living someone else's life. The person I thought I was had left the building a long time ago. It horrified me that my children were now viewing the movie I had watched as a child—witnessing parents physically assaulting each other. I had to start the process of breaking this chain of destruction, or my children were going to grow up living these habits, hurts, and hang-ups all over again! Somehow, I had to halt the violence.

The attention I received from Jonathan taught me that I deserved better, and through him I was able to gain the confidence to realize I wanted to be treated better!

I found myself facing the proverbial fork in the road.

18

Of Love and War and Everything In Between

One evening I went to my friend James' house with the intention of discussing business. He had been working on graphics for my book. I listened to him distractedly as he laid out his ideas for the interior design.

"Hey, where are you?" he asked.

"I'm sorry, James. I'm just tired."

"Are you sure that there isn't something bothering you."

I knew that James was a recovering alcoholic and debated whether or not to level with him about my addiction problems. He had been very up front with me several months earlier about the difficulties that drinking had caused his marriage. What did I have to lose?

"I think I'm an alcoholic, and that scares the shit out of me."

He looked startled but recovered quickly.

"It is very frightening, I know," he consoled.

"Do you think I'm an alcoholic," I timidly asked, fearing his response.

Instead of answering my question, he opened a big blue book that was resting on the end table, and together we read the description of an alcoholic. I wasn't able to comprehend much of what he read, but I had to admit that there were passages that felt all too familiar.

"Let's go to a meeting tonight," James proposed.

"Now! I can't do that!"

"Why not?"

"I drank earlier," I confessed.

"That's okay."

I looked at his expectant face, took a deep breath, and reluctantly agreed to go.

A half-hour later I had settled myself into the darkest corner of a florescent-lit church basement. A prosperous looking middle-aged man was introduced and the room applauded. He told a humorous tale of his rise up the ladder to become a wealthy Wall Street broker and the rapid descent when his addiction to alcohol and drugs overwhelmed his life. I found myself engaged and laughing. *How could there be so much humor in something so devastating?*

After the meeting, I decided that I would give up drinking the following day. Meanwhile, I bought a gallon of wine to treat myself to one last hurrah.

I called my sister Sandra. She was surprised to hear from me. After my father's funeral, the family had disintegrated. It was too painful to be in each other's company. I hadn't spoken to Sandra very often over the past ten years, but I knew that she and my brother Stevie were both members of Alcoholics Anonymous.

"I think you're full of shit," was Sandy's first response when I told her that I thought I was an alcoholic. "Is this one of your games? You sound drunk."

I started crying and talking about how difficult my life had become. "I'm drinking a lot every day. I can't seem to stop. I don't know what to do."

Sandra's voice softened. "It's going to be okay, Christa. I've been in AA for three years and it's a wonderful program. Go to meetings," she advised, "and for God's sake, for the first time in your life, listen!"

The next morning I was no longer convinced that I was an alcoholic, but I went to see my therapist to talk about the drinking. She helped me admit that my life was unmanageable and suggested that I enter a rehab facility. After my appointment, I knew that it was time to face myself.

Robert was ten and Richard was five, and I couldn't stand to look at their sad faces as their mother fell apart before their eyes. "I just want you to be happy, Mommy," Richard had said to me the week earlier as he tried to comfort me following an argument with Jacob. I was in a panic over the trauma being inflicted on my children.

"You want to stop drinking now?" Jacob scoffed as he chugged a beer. "It's the busiest time of the summer? You'll never do it." I explained that my therapist suggested that I check into a rehab that would cost $300 a night. His anger flared, a sure sign that violence could strike at any moment. I turned my back, walked away, slipped into our bedroom, and started to pray. I knew my life was treading on thin ice.

We couldn't afford a rehab, according to Jacob, so I began attending AA meetings regularly. Jacob was dumbfounded at the turn of events and not interested in hearing anything about my new direction in life. He feared losing control of his best drinking buddy. This was an extreme red flag, warning me that my sobriety would not come easily.

I would lie awake for hours going over the wreckage of my marriage. The euphoric sensations of alcohol had lulled me into a fantasy that everything would work out between us in the end. Slowly, I was coming out of a trance and gaining a more accurate perspective on the events and relationships in my life.

Tucked at the back of my mind through all of these circumstances was a lingering obsession with Jonathan. I had no idea if he returned my feelings and decided it was time to find out.

It was the beginning of September when I drove to North Haven at Jonathan's request. There was his sunny disposition, the big kiss, and the hug hello. "How've you been?" he enthused. "I've missed you."

"I've missed you too," I said as evenly as possible

as I observed him very closely. "Can we talk?"

"Certainly, Christa, my dear." He led the way to our usual spot on the dock. I took in a gulp of air and looked out over the bay as I launched into a do-or-die confession.

"You are on my mind all of the time. You're with me during the day and in my dreams at night. I am head over heels in love with you." I looked at Jonathan, and although he seemed surprised, I didn't think he was about to run off screaming in horror. I continued. "Our interests, in flowers, artwork, music, sailing, and even politics, are so much the same. I feel so at ease when I am with you."

"Christa, darling, we can't be lovers," he said, as he looked me squarely in the eyes. "It will ruin our business relationship. I want you to keep working for me. I want to keep creating with you. I want to be your friend. I am sorry if I had led you on."

"You didn't lead me on," I said, as the heat of mortification burned in my heart. "I just want you to know how I feel."

I'm an artist," he explained, "a photographer. I'm on the go all the time. You're married. You have children."

"There's no big secret where my marriage is right now. You've known that all along. What does your traveling have to do with the way I feel about you, and the way I think you feel about me?"

For a moment, an intense energy passed between us. Then he turned his head and said, "I think we should go back into the house, sit down, and finish our conversation about your work."

I had been utterly rejected and went into a mild shock. I honestly had not anticipated his reaction. He had carried on so—hugs, late night phone calls, compliments—that I assumed that he had feelings for me. We had never been physically intimate, except for holding each other's arms as we walked around the estate. I looked out over the water at his sailboat as we went back into the house. By the time we arrived in the living room, Jonathan's disposition had changed. He was all business.

"Have you got my bill?"

"Not at the moment," I answered.

"I have to have some idea of what I owe you before we proceed," he pushed.

I was desperately holding in my tears, knowing that if I let loose there would be no stopping them. "I'm waiting for an estimate on work that was contracted out. It will be just a few days."

I have made a complete fool of myself.

Jonathan switched gears again complimenting me on the beautiful work. I had to get out of there. I couldn't look at him.

"Christa, darling, please send me my bill. I want to make sure it is cleared up before I leave."

I turned around in surprise, "You're leaving?"

"I wanted to tell you today. That's one of the reasons that I asked you to come over. I'm going on an eighteen-month photo shoot in Europe. It doesn't look like I'll be here next summer at all. I wanted to talk to you about what maintenance needed to be taken care of."

I could feel my heart sliding into a terrible, frightening place. If I had done things differently, had said the right word, had said no words at all, I wouldn't be feeling this arrow of abandonment shooting through my heart.

As I was leaving, his phone rang. I could hear a woman on the other end confirming their date that night. He was laughing and giggling and being his charming self.

I got in my truck and fumbled with the keys, dropping them twice on the floor, and then with damp, trembling hands, turned the ignition as quickly as possible. Jonathan came running out of the house and called to me in a business tone. "I'll contact you," he said. I felt as if the universe had just tossed me out of its orbit. I drove away.

I parked at Long Beach and sat in my truck looking at the water, sobbing my head off. I had been sober for three weeks and kept asking myself why had I sobered up in the first place? I desperately wanted a drink. I could taste the wine.

A spectacular sunset was forming on the horizon. The distraction that Jonathan had provided for months was gone, and I was left alone with a husband I didn't know anymore.

I'll just have one glass of wine.

I started up the truck and let it take me to the liquor store.

19

Calling All Angels

"Can we talk?" I asked quietly as Jacob stirred in bed the morning after a heavy night of drinking.

"No thanks," he answered definitively as he rose and began putting on a pair of jeans that lay on the chair.

"We can't go on like this," I pleaded.

"Like what!" he snapped. "There's no problem this morning, unless you've decided to create one."

"Jacob, please, we need to be a sober family. Please come to a meeting with me. It's our only chance."

"Christa's latest obsession!" he mocked me. "What we need is for you to have a little love and consideration for someone other than yourself."

He walked out. I lay in the bed and listened to him get into his truck and drive away.

If only Jacob would get straight, it would enable

me to get back on the sober trail. After my Jonathan debacle, I had begun a pattern of slipping. Jacob had done everything he could to undermine my effort to stay sober and it was succeeding. I attended AA meetings and afterwards drank in secret at the American Hotel.

I was barely able to think straight on a day-to-day basis. My entire dizzying life crowded in on me. Never in my life had I found any real happiness.

I took a long walk out on the beach and screamed at the top of my lungs: WHY CAN'T YOU SHOW ME A SOFTER WAY! I CAN'T BELIEVE THAT YOU WANT ME TO LIVE IN THIS PAIN AND SUFFERING! When I exhausted myself, a voice said to me, *"Christa, you are loved and always have been. Allow me to love you."* I felt this intense warmth spread through my body. For that moment, for the first time in my life, I felt safe.

In the grips of my alcoholism, I was close to spiritual death. I began attending a church for the first time in thirty-five years in search of spiritual direction. I had heard good things about the new Pastor and his wife, just arrived missionaries from Ecuador. Through them I learned about a God of second chances. This stirred a sense of divine spirit that filled the empty void in my life with a power of love. I started to become quieter in my thinking and move from my heart.

The alcohol recovery program requires the addict to put their faith in a higher power of their choosing. Although I was still drinking, I was beginning to understand that many of my problems stemmed from the sheer strength of my self-will. The acceptance of my powerlessness over the people and events in my life was the ticket to freedom.

Eugene had a sprawling home on the ocean off Potato Road in Bridgehampton and became a client in 1979. He owned a construction company in the city and had millions. Eugene seemed moved by my dedication to his property; and in my mind, I thought we had a good working relationship. He was very generous with tips and bonuses and sent many compliments and referrals my way.

I was in tight financial shape and decided to ask Eugene for an advance. In a heartfelt conversation I spilled my guts about the difficulties at home and my attempts at recovery, assuming that our relationship of twenty-four years would allow me to confide in him. Eugene had seemed happy with my work, and I felt my job was virtually guaranteed.

His response blew me away. Shockingly, there would be no advance, and for good measure, my services were terminated on the spot.

"You fucked it up again!" Jacob proclaimed. "What were you thinking? What in your mind made you tell a client that you're a boozehound? It doesn't matter if you're sober or drunk; you're just a fuck up."

I hated the fact that he was right. My thinking was skewered. I couldn't get it through my head that as long as I continued to pick up a drink, my life would be unmanageable. The disease convinced me that I could drink one glass of wine on Saturday nights. The following weekend, I allowed myself two glasses of wine on Saturday night, and by the third weekend, I figured I could drink both Saturday and Sunday nights. Before I knew it, wine on Wednesday or Thursday seemed like a good way to break up the week. The bottom soon fell out and I was again a full-blown active alcoholic.

The week before Easter we were hammered by a severe snowstorm. "That's it," I declared, "I'm packing the kids up. There's a three-foot base up at Hunter Mountain." Upstate had just measured seven inches of new snow, and I needed to get away.

We stopped to see my mother who was in a nursing home not far from the ski lodge. Jeanne hated the place, preferring to live in her house in Kingston, but was not capable of caring for herself. My mother visited with the boys for a while, and then I wheeled her through the corridors.

Despite her condition, she was still very perceptive and could see that I was having a difficult time.

"What's wrong? You look like hell?"

"Nothings wrong. I'm just tired."

I tried to evade her scrutiny but she wasn't buying it. She pushed her wheel chair into the common room and directed me to take a seat.

"Christa," she said, "you and I have a way of doing things the hard way. I can tell that something is wrong. How are things going with the booze?"

"Mom, I can't lie to you; it's not going well. I can't stay stopped."

I sadly looked at her.

"You're stubborn, like me, but you can do it. I didn't have a chance in my life until I put down the drink. What about Jacob?"

"He's doing everything possible to sabotage my effort to stop."

"I remember that smell, sleeping next to your father," she consoled. "It was difficult." She got really quiet. "He's not still hitting you, is he?"

"Yes," I answered quietly.

"Christa, you owe it to your boys to put an end to this. It is not good for them to grow up in that atmosphere. I lose sleep at night over the memories of having put you kids through so much of that."

My mother started to sob. I put my arms around her and began to cry as well. The sorrow of two generations of alcoholism poured through our tears. I had become my mother, and it was frightening.

She composed herself and spoke. "God promised me that the family would heal someday, although I won't live to see it. Believing that you will all be okay is what keeps me going."

"Don't worry, Ma."

"You can't run from your problems," she pleaded. "I tried. You have to stop drinking. You have to break the chain."

I didn't respond, but I knew she was right.

There was one more stop before the slopes, my father's grave. It had been fourteen years since my last visit.

"How old was Grandpa when he died," asked Richard as we stood over the gravestone.

"Sixty-two," I responded.

"That's old, right?"

"Not really."

"Why did he die?" he continued.

I hesitated for a beat, and then gave him the whitewashed answer to that question. "He was in the hospital having some tests, and somebody gave him the wrong medicine and he had a very bad reaction to it." Richard listened to my explanation with a somber acceptance.

Later as the boys and I rode the ski lift, Richard shouted, "Mom, look over there. There's a grave."

When we reached the top of the mountain, Richard skied in the direction of the gravesite and I followed. As we looked at the tombstone, he asked, "How old was he?"

"Ninety-eight."

"Wow, he lived a lot longer than Grandpa."

"Look," I said, "it says he skied Hunter his whole life and died of a heart attack right here on the mountain."

Looking at that tombstone with my son, I had my moment of undeniable truth: *My father died of alcoholism*. And here was a man who followed his dreams and died of a heart attack at ninety-eight while skiing. *Follow your dreams and your passion; you live. When you drink, you die.*

I decided to go out in my customary blaze of glory and had my last big drunken bash the next day. By mid afternoon I had consumed two gallons of cheap wine. I felt sick and tired of being sick and tired. Willpower wasn't going to get me sober. I had to hand it over. DEAR LORD, DO WITH ME AS YOU WISH. I AM NO LONGER CAPABLE OF HANDLING THIS MYSELF.

The enormity of getting sober hadn't quite hit me. I had to learn how to confront my feelings without the buffer of alcohol and drugs. I needed all the help that I could get. I began to go to several meetings a day and reach out to other recovering alcoholics. At every turn I was met with love, compassion, and understanding. I had been attending church regularly and slowly making a stronger connection with a power greater than myself.

I went to a weekend conference in Bushkill, Pennsylvania, with the Hampton Alliance Missionary Women. One of the featured speakers was a beautiful former beauty queen by the name of Katrina who had written a book called *Married to Mohammed*. Katrina had been Miss Alabama before marrying a Muslim. In her fourteen-year marriage, she had four children and lived an Islamic life, flying back and forth between Syria and Iraq.

I was transfixed as Katrina talked about her marriage. Her husband had plenty of money, which helped to disguise the fact that he was an abusive man. Materialism had helped warp her perceptions and enticed her into accepting a lifestyle that was physically and mentally intolerable.

Her story hit me right in my heart and mind. It

was my story. I had stayed faithful to my husband for twenty-four years directly due to my dependency on the money. Jacob helped provide a lifestyle that I had become very accustomed to, so what if I was getting physically and emotionally beaten up in the process. For two and a half days I listened to Katrina and literally shook in my boots.

My mother was diagnosed with cancer of the larynx in the fall of 2003. Her doctors advised against treatment believing that she was not strong enough to survive chemo. But my mother had her own ideas.

"I've always been curious about chemo and radiation," she said as an explanation for going against doctor's advice.

I researched her condition thoroughly and had come to the conclusion that her doctors knew what they were talking about and pleaded with my mother to reconsider. She was unmovable.

Jeanne's way finally caught up with my mother. After her second treatment she had a massive heart attack and died at the age of eighty-two. The triplets were inconsolable at the funeral. They had been heavily drugged, but that didn't take the edge off of their hysteria. Sandra, Stevie, and I were all sober but not able to overcome the distance between us. The wounds were still open. We got through my mother's service and retreated to our separate lives.

20

Shelter From the Storm

As the planting season began I was clean and sober. I thought that an alcohol-free Christa would guarantee a saner, more orderly life, but I was mistaken. I might have changed, but the circus around me continued on as usual.

The work was high pressured, the clients very demanding. My children had their needs to be met, and my turbulent relationship with Jacob had to be resolved. It was often overwhelming. The only certainty in my day was that I couldn't pick up a drink.

Several weeks into sobriety, there was a message on my voice mail from Jonathan. He had returned to the East End, deciding to forego his assignment in Europe with the start of the war in Iraq. I got heart palpitations when I heard his cheerful voice.

After several messages, I finally called him back. He seemed anxious to see me, and we made an appointment to get together. I knew I was in the danger zone but couldn't stop myself.

Maybe there is a chance!

It was a rainy Saturday afternoon as I pulled into the North Haven estate. Jonathan greeted me with enthusiasm and a hug. We settled on a couch overlooking the bay window views and caught up on our lives. It was wonderful to be with him, and I was thoroughly enjoying the moment. The conversation turned to business, and I rolled out a plan to show him my latest design for his garden. He placed his hand on the coffee table to get a closer look, and I noticed that there was a wedding ring on his finger.

"Oh, my gosh! You got married! That's a wedding ring! You got married!" I heard my voice sounding scratchy and whiny.

He laughed uncomfortably and handed me the blueprint.

I felt panicky. "I gotta go," I said, barely breathing. I needed to get home quickly.

"Listen, I'll give you a call," he said. "I want to talk to you about some ideas I had when I was down in Puerto Rico?"

I was rushing and awkwardly dropped my pocketbook. *Get me out of here!* The contents emptied on the floor, and we both bent over to gather my personal stuff. I wanted to offer congratulations, but they just wouldn't come. Finally, I managed to say,

"Let's talk next week," and fled.

Once again, I parked at Long Beach, my favorite place to go when reality hits me squarely in the head. My phone rang incessantly, bombarding with calls from Jacob. Finally, I answered.

"God Damn it, Christa, get your fucking ass home!"

I CAN'T LIVE LIKE THIS ANYMORE. I CAN'T STAY AWAY FROM A DRINK WHEN HE TREATS ME LIKE THIS!

I sat quietly looking at the ocean and knew that I couldn't go on anymore. Something had to give.

Although Jacob and I had gone our separate ways in operating the business, the money still went into one pot. I handed over the checks from my clients, and Jacob deposited them into a business account that he controlled. In order to have access to cash, I had my clients mail checks to a personal post office box, and I would withhold small sums to cover my personal expenses. Jacob was aware of this arrangement and had not objected. But as my sobriety grew, he became suspicious of what I was doing.

His focus was centered on a check that I'd been expecting from my mother's estate. Her house had been sold, and I was to share in the proceeds with my siblings. Sandra was the executor and responsible for distributing the money.

Jacob was frantic over the recent loss of a major client. This had put a huge gap in his finances, and he was looking for that check. Everyday he asked about it, and I assured him that the funds hadn't been released. As the pressure built on Jacob, he stayed on me for the money as I danced around his inquiries.

One night I arrived home from a meeting to find Jacob drunk and belligerent.

"I want that check!" he slurred. "Where is it?"

"Sandra says we'll have it in a couple of weeks," I offered.

"You're a liar!" he screamed and ran upstairs to our bedroom. I followed him and watched as he began searching my drawers, flinging articles of clothing everywhere.

"You bastard!" I screamed. "There is no check!"

"I don't believe you."

He grabbed me by the arm and threw me on the bed. He approached me with that dangerous look. I put my feet up against his chest and our eyes connected in a flaming lock.

I threatened, "I'm going to leave you, you miserable motherfucker!"

He pulled my legs, flipped me over and whacked me in the rear. "Don't come downstairs tonight!" he ordered and left the room.

I stayed there seething in anger until I became aware of Richard standing by the bed. He was crying, and I pulled him close to me.

"Why are you and daddy always yelling?" he asked.

I held him tightly and knew then and there that I was leaving. That night, I began to plot my getaway. I was terrified and got down on my knees in prayer. I reached for the higher power that had begun to offer safe harbor for my fear.

PLEASE GOD...I KNOW I HAVE TO GET AWAY, BUT I CAN'T DO THIS ALONE. I AM SO FRIGHTENED! YOU HAVE TO SHOW ME THE WAY!

I awoke at dawn, unafraid and filled with grace. Something in me had changed. I knew everything was going to be okay, as long as I surrendered and let God do for me what I could not do for myself.

Later that morning, I called a friend at Brown Harris Stevens Real Estate. It was late June, the height of the tourist season, an impossible time to rent year round. "I have only one house," she said. "Come on over and we'll have a look."

It was perfect—4 an upside-down house in Sag Harbor with a fabulous view of the Peconic Bay and a thousand-acre land reserve. But it was too expensive. Several conversations with the landlord that week ended with me hanging up on him in disgust. Finally, he relented on the rent, dropping the price from exorbitant to over-priced, and we made a deal.

Sandra had been holding the funds from my mother's estate, awaiting word of where they should be sent. I called her and had the $25,000 check put in overnight mail to my post office box. The house was secured.

Time accelerated. I bought a new cell phone and bedroom set and began to carefully move my things, one item at a time. I was waiting until mid-July when I would send the children to a sleep-away camp before making the big move.

The day finally arrived. It was a Wednesday, and Jacob was to spend the day working in Water Mill. I rented two white paneled trucks and drove over to an area in Southampton, where you could hire day workers. I selected six men, and we drove the trucks to a cul-de-sac not far from my house. I instructed them to wait until I called for them.

When I returned home, I was surprised to find Jacob coming out of the shower. He normally left for the day at 10:00, but he had decided to delay his departure. He went into the kitchen and sat down with a cup of tea and the newspaper. I had to conceal my adrenaline that was pumping madly.

"Aren't you going to work?" I asked, trying to sound casual.

"Eventually," he answered as he lit a cigarette.

I went upstairs to wait, trying to stay out of his way. The clock slowed down as Jacob muddled about with a number of odd tasks. When I heard him tuning his guitar, I went downstairs. He was in a good mood.

"Listen to this piece I've been working on."

He began to play, and it was agonizing for me to engage in supportive banter.

"Have you cancelled work today?" I prodded.

His antenna went up. "Why are you here?" he asked suspiciously.

"I'm waiting for a phone call."

Finally, he went upstairs to get ready. I called my workers and told them to stay alert.

Jacob came downstairs dressed for work. "Since the kids are away, maybe we can do something tonight," he offered.

"That would be fun," I lied.

"See you later," he said as he walked out the door, not knowing that everything was about to change.

The workers moved in, and we quickly began to load the trucks with enough furniture and household items to set up my new home comfortably. It was terrifying and thrilling. I was a nervous wreck, watching for any sign of Jacob's return. With the trucks filled, the movers pulled away, leaving me alone. I walked through the house that now had dust prints where the furniture once stood.

I went into my bedroom and sat on the bed where Jacob and I had created our children. How could I have loved someone as much as I had loved Jacob and have it turn into such an unbearable stalemate? He had no awareness that morning that he was about to lose his family. Jacob loved his children and would be devastated to return to an empty house.

I cried for us all. Alcoholism had obscured our judgment of what was really important. The disease had existed in my family and in Jacob's for generations. I wanted to stop the cycle of anger, violence, and alcohol. I did not want my children to take on the baggage that had been handed down to the adults in their life.

I walked through the house one more time and out the door. The sun seemed to be a little brighter and the sky a little bluer. Out of the corner of my eye

I spotted a magnificent Western Bluebird. I took the moment to really see the creature, and in that moment I was filled with the hope of a better life to come if I remained sober and true to myself and available to the God of my understanding.

Epilogue

February 3, 2007

Today, on my fiftieth birthday, I'm grateful to have a second chance at life. I left Jacob in 2004. The toxic poisons endangered my children and threatened my sanity. Soon I will celebrate four years of sobriety. It has been a miracle and the most heart-wrenching time of my life. As my vision cleared I was forced to open the denial file, and the truth has often been harsh and painful. But it was the beginning of healing.

I sought a therapist and for the first time in thirty years admitted that I was raped as a girl. Allowing myself to be a victim of domestic abuse could be tied to an early loss of power at the hands of my school-teacher. I was fortunate to have a career, since most women who escape violent marriages leave without even a checkbook. My business continues to thrive and has allowed me to sustain my independence. For the first time, I am managing my own money and developing a financial plan for the future.

My family of origin is alive and well. After my mother's death, her prediction that the family would heal one day came to pass. My siblings are close today. We often compare notes about our childhoods and are able to look back with a sense of humor. The triplets are the glue that keeps us together. As I've come to know them as adults, I appreciate the wonderful women they are and realize that my mother put too much focus on their handicaps, rather than their gifts. Having worked through the painful memories, we finally have love, joy, and laughter amongst us.

The boys are well. Robert is a deep thinker and philosopher; Richard is a great athlete and student. My mother was right; they enrich my life with joy and love.

Jacob is still suffering from the disease of alcoholism. Every day I pray for his deliverance, so that he might become the father that my boys deserve. There will always be a part of me who looks off in the distance, hoping to see that cowboy who lassoed my heart twenty-five-years ago, become a healed man.

I have become a Christian and I am dedicated to helping and serving God and the less fortunate. Through my faith and trust, I have been given a life that is beyond my wildest hopes and dreams. I am so lucky to have been able to rely and trust that a good God has always been watching over me.

The Serenity Prayer

God grant me the Serenity
to accept the things I cannot change,
Courage to change the things I can,
And the Wisdom to know the difference.
Living one day at a time;
Enjoying one moment at a time;
Accepting hardships as the pathway to peace;
Taking, as Jesus did, this sinful world as it is,
not as I would have it;
Trusting that He will make all things
right if I surrender to His Will;
That I may be reasonably happy in this life
and supremely happy with Him
Forever in the next.
Amen
~ Reinhold Niebuhr

Trust in the LORD with all your heart
and lean not on your own understanding;
in all your ways acknowledge him,
and he will direct your paths.

Proverbs 3, 5-6

Third Step Prayer

God, I offer myself to you—to build with me
and to do with me as you will. Relieve me of the
bondage of self, that I may better do your will.
Take away my difficulties, that victory over them
may bear witness to those I would help of your
power, your love, and your way of life. May I do
your will always.

About the Author

Finding Spirituality is not a geographical thing, as discovered by someone whose childhood was filled with more questions than answers. The youngest of six, growing up with triplet sisters, all born with Cerebral Palsy, Christa Jan Ryan's candid and personal journey winds back and forth from Kingston, New York, to the fabulous Hamptons and into a journey of self discovery and transformation.

As a landscaper to the rich and famous, her story is filled with humor and revelations that match her powerful self-will with that of God's far more subtle ways, only to realize that His Grace is upon all of us. We only have to reach out and accept it.

The Author lives in New York with her two sons and their cats, Posh and Pumpkin.

EMPOWERING BOOKS FOR WOMEN

> *Call in your order for fast service and quantity discounts!*
> **(541) 347- 9882**

OR order on-line at **www.rdrpublishers.com** *using PayPal.*
OR order by FAX at **(541) 347-9883** *OR by mail:*
Make a copy of this form; enclose payment information:

Robert D. Reed Publishers
1380 Face Rock Drive, Bandon, OR 97411

Name: _____

Address: _____

City: _____ State: _____ Zip: _____

Phone: _____ Fax: _____ Cell: _____

E-Mail: _____

Payment by check /_/ or credit card /_/ *(All major credit cards are accepted.)*

Name on card: _____

Card Number: _____

Exp. Date _____ Last 3-Digit number on back of card: _____

		Quantity	Total Amount
Silent Screams from the Hamptons			
by Christa Jan Ryan........................	$15.95	_____	_____
Scared to Leave, Afraid to Stay			
by Barry Goldstein	$24.95	_____	_____
The 86th Degree			
by Barbara Harken	$14.95	_____	_____
Liberty's Quest			
by Liberty Kovacs	$29.95	_____	_____
Out of the Cocoon			
by Brenda Lee.................................	$14.95	_____	_____
Silver Dreams			
by Sondra Rice Newman	$24.95	_____	_____
Stefi			
by Jenny Paschall	$22.95	_____	_____

Quantity of books ordered: _____ Total amount for books: _____

Shipping is $3.50 1st book + $1 for each additional book. Plus postage: _____

FINAL TOTAL: _____